Marshall Versus Jefferson:
The Political Background of *Marbury* v. *Madison*

❧ BORZOI SERIES ❧
IN
UNITED STATES
CONSTITUTIONAL HISTORY

CONSULTING EDITOR:
PAUL MURPHY

UNIVERSITY OF MINNESOTA

Marshall Versus Jefferson:
The Political Background of Marbury v. Madison

DONALD O. DEWEY

CALIFORNIA STATE COLLEGE, LOS ANGELES

ALFRED · A · KNOPF   NEW YORK

FOR

Charlotte

[*Marbury* v. *Madison*] has been shorn of all but its historical importance and stands as a warning to those who would attempt to expound the rules of constitutional law simply through a process of analytical reasoning, ignoring the very important contributions of economics and of politics.

[J. A. C. Grant—"Marbury v. Madison Today," *American Political Science Review,* XXIII (1929) , 681]

❧ Preface ❧

John Marshall left so few personal letters and documents behind that he is known largely through his judicial decisions. Yet the decision for which he is best known, *Marbury* v. *Madison*, tells little about Marshall or the interpersonal and political forces underlying the decision. Late in life, Marshall himself remarked cryptically that the only possible mystery in his lifelong conflict with Thomas Jefferson was the decision to go into the *Marbury* case in such depth. "Nothing is unknown or can be misunderstood by intelligent men," Marshall wrote in 1830, "unless it be the motives which compelled the court to give its opinion at large on the case of Marbury vs Madison." All too characteristically, Marshall provided only an introduction to this mystery, no conclusion. This book is not the explanation that Marshall would have offered, but shows, instead, why Marshall might have preferred for it to remain a mystery.

I have been constantly indebted to the staff of The Henry E. Huntington Library throughout my work on this volume. Stephen G. Kurtz and Herbert A. Johnson of The Papers of John Marshall, and John C. Dann of The College of William and Mary, have been generous with their assistance. At California State College, Los Angeles, the Faculty Awards Committee and the John F. Kennedy Library have also given valuable assistance. Paul L. Murphy of the University of Minnesota and Mrs. June Fischbein of Alfred A. Knopf, Inc., contributed much to the conversion of a manuscript into a book. Finally, and most importantly, I have been the grateful beneficiary of wise counsel and infinite patience from my wife, Charlotte Neuber Dewey.

San Gabriel, California   Donald O. Dewey

❧ Contents ❧

10

Marshall Versus Jefferson:
The Political Background of *Marbury* v. *Madison*

❦ 1 ❧

ADAMS FINDS
CHIEF JUSTICE

———————————◆———————————

On January 20, 1801, just six weeks before he left the presidency, John Adams astonished the Senate by nominating John Marshall of Virginia as chief justice of the United States Supreme Court. The Senate was no more surprised than the rest of the country, however, for the elevation of secretary of state Marshall to the supreme bench seems to have occurred to no one but John Adams; and Adams himself had leaned toward three other possibilities—John Jay, William Cushing, and William Paterson—until the very day that he asked Marshall to serve.

The appointment of any one of the other three men would have been a less surprising, and surely less effective, legacy for the retiring President to bequeath to the Jefferson administration. As a sidelight of a long and impressive political and diplomatic career, John Jay had been the first chief judge of the state of New York, and he had served from 1789 to 1795 as the first chief justice during the important formative years of the United States Supreme Court. When Adams appointed Jay to his old position on the bench on December 19, 1800, the Federalist Senate happily and speedily confirmed him—Jay refused to serve, though, citing his discontent with the judicial system and his own ailing health.

Adams thought seriously about appointing William Cushing, a personal friend from Massachusetts and the senior justice of the Supreme Court. Cushing, who came from a long line of royal judges, had been on the Supreme Court since its inception in 1789 and had served for seventeen years prior to that on the Massachusetts Superior Court. Now, however, he was nearly seventy years old and could not be relied upon to hold his seat until some future Federalist President could name a successor; besides, Cushing had already declined the chief justiceship in 1796 because of ill health.

William Paterson was a healthier specimen, but at the eleventh hour Adams became irrevocably opposed to his advancement, either because the Hamiltonian Federalists so desperately wanted the appointment for him or because Adams hesitated to hurt Cushing by boosting one of his brethren past him. Although Paterson's credentials were impressive, Adams chose not to read them. Paterson had been a significant co-author of the Constitution and the Judiciary Act of 1789, which established the federal judiciary and defined its jurisdiction. He had then served as an associate justice of the Supreme Court since 1793.

Advancing either Cushing or Paterson would have created a vacancy on the court which would have to be filled hastily by a deserving Federalist. Yet Marshall was not even considered for this lower position. Through most of the month of January 1801, the President's son, Thomas, was persistently wooing Jared Ingersoll of Philadelphia to accept the anticipated vacancy. At fifty-one, Ingersoll was only four years younger than Jay and Paterson. He was United States district attorney in Pennsylvania and one of the best of a bumper crop of Philadelphia lawyers. He had served in the Continental Congress as early as 1780 and was one of the relatively silent members of the Convention of 1787, where the United States Constitution was drawn up.

MARSHALL'S QUALIFICATIONS

In legal, and especially judicial, experience John Marshall compared unfavorably with all the foregoing. He possessed very real strengths, to be sure, but these strengths were not those of the traditional jurist. Louis Boudin is, characteristically, overly severe with Marshall when he complains that his legal education "was of the scantiest imaginable; and there is no proof of his ever having improved very much on his original education by subsequent study." There is no question, however, that Marshall was more a politician than a legal scholar. Even so, he was so successful in his twelve years of legal practice that Attorney General Charles Lee informed President Washington in 1796 that Marshall was "at the head of his profession in Virginia."

Besides his faithful service to President Adams in Congress and as secretary of state, at a time when Adams could find few Federalists whom he could trust, Marshall's qualifications for the Supreme Court were peculiarly physical. Most important, he was a young and vigorous member of a political party which had become too much of a haven for old men, especially wealthy old men from New England. His anomalous position as a Federalist in Thomas Jefferson's private domain of Virginia could conceivably make Marshall a foundation on which a rejuvenated national party might be erected. In any event, his longstanding antagonism for Jefferson would make Marshall's advancement to a lifetime position in Washington, D.C., unpleasant medicine for the incoming President. This would have been no small consideration to a man who was one of only two Presidents (both of them Adamses) who were so bitter about their defeat that they refused to remain behind to see their successors safely inaugurated.

Finally, Marshall was in daily contact with Adams in the cabinet, so that no time would be squandered by correspondence and mail delays. Politics dictated an immediate appointment, and Adams knew that he could count on a decisive answer from Marshall—either to accept or reject the office without wasting precious time. Adams had waited more than two weeks for Jay's refusal from New York; Cushing might have delayed for weeks longer, and Ingersoll in Philadelphia was being either coy or indecisive about his intentions. This, when there was no time to waste! Congress was on the verge of changing the number of Supreme Court justices from six to five. Unless Adams acted promptly, he (rather than Jefferson, as was intended) might be deprived of the opportunity of filling the sixth position on the Supreme Court with his own appointee. From Marshall, Adams could, and did, get a direct answer on January 19.

Marshall was as surprised as any Federalist senator (though more pleasantly so) when Adams turned to him. Once the triumph of Jefferson's Republican party in 1800 was certain, Marshall had happily anticipated the resumption of his legal practice in Richmond, Virginia. Writing to Adams' defeated running mate, Charles Cotesworth Pinckney, on December 18, 1800, Marshall had remarked that "If my present wish can succeed so far as respects myself I shall never again fill any political station whatever." He had also speculated on the likelihood of Jay's refusal to resume the judicial robes, adding a "fear [that] the President will nominate the senior Judge [Cushing] to that office." Marshall had feared the political risks of Cushing's advancement. He had not even dreamed of any personal competition with Cushing. In fact, on the very day that Marshall was asked to become chief justice, he claims that he urged the appointment of William Paterson.

The dumbfounded Senate delayed action on Marshall's nomination until January 27, when Federalist senators finally recognized that Adams would not withdraw the nomination and that if they rejected Marshall they were, in effect, leaving the appointment open to Jefferson. Unenthused as they were at the nomination of Marshall, they still felt he was preferable to anyone Jefferson might name. Thus it was not until the last day of January that the new secretary of war, Samuel Dexter, momentarily became acting secretary of state to sign Marshall's commission as chief justice. Four days later, when the "Marshall Court" convened for the first time, Marshall wrote Adams to announce his formal acceptance of the office, adding his desire "never to give you occasion to regret having made this appointment." For the moment Adams made only a polite response, adding that he wanted Marshall also to continue as secretary of state for the month of Adams' administration which remained. A quarter of a century later, Adams asserted more pride in the nomination than was evident in 1801, when he told Marshall's son that "My gift of John Marshall to the people of the United States was the proudest act of my life."

Although Marshall's appointment in 1801 appears to have been an impulsive act, President Adams had long respected the lanky Virginian and had asked him to serve in a number of high offices. In 1797 he appointed Marshall, Charles C. Pinckney, and Elbridge Gerry to the so-called XYZ mission to negotiate with the French Directory. Even though this mission ran aground against corrupt French agents, Marshall returned to the applause of the American people and the praise of John Adams. Convinced that "of the three envoys, the conduct of Marshall alone has been entirely satisfactory, and ought to be marked by the most decided approbation of the public," Adams decided in 1798 that Marshall should succeed the late James Wilson on the Supreme Court. When Marshall declined, the appointment went to his close friend, Bushrod Washington. Marshall went, instead to the House of Representatives, at the insistence of George Washington. In May 1800 Marshall was actually appointed and confirmed as secretary of war before rejecting the position. A week later, Marshall was asked to become secretary of state when Adams dismissed High Federalists from his cabinet. This time he accepted because "the office was precisely that which I wished, and for which I had vanity enough to think myself fitted." Furthermore, the appointment relieved him of the burden of running again for Congress.

FEDERALIST VIEW OF MARSHALL

Few Federalist leaders and, of course, no Republicans shared John Adams' enthusiasm for Marshall in 1801. Marshall had been immensely popular, especially among Federalists, when he returned from the abortive XYZ mission; he was one of those rare diplomats who wins glory from failure. Nevertheless, his independence during his brief tenure in the House of Representatives soon earned him the distrust of the "High Federalists," those who looked to Alexander Hamilton rather than to John Adams for leadership. Marshall demonstrated a spirit of moderation and common sense at a time when neither was common within the Federalist hierarchy. He supported Adams' efforts to restore peace with France, even becoming secretary of state when Adams finally removed the hawkish Timothy Pickering, who was doing his best to hamper the pursuit of peace. Marshall's protests and amendments also prevented the Federalist-dominated Congress from shoving through a Disputed Elections Bill in 1800 which would have given to a congressional committee (safely Federalist, of course) final authority in canvassing the electoral vote for President. Marshall's obstinance in this case might have made possible the election of Thomas Jefferson; at any rate, some Federalists were prepared to discredit Marshall with this achievement. Prior to Marshall's revolt, Speaker Theodore Sedgwick had been confident that the Disputed Elections Bill would "succeed & secure us against [the Republicans'] designs."

Marshall's greatest affront to pure Federalism came during his congressional campaign of 1799 when he criticized the Alien and Sedition Acts, legislation which marked the capstone of Federalist designs to stifle dissent. Marshall protested the expediency of these laws in a campaign document. Although he did not regard them as unconstitutional or "fraught with all those mischiefs ascribed to them as inimical to freedom," he dismissed them as useless measures "calculated to create unnecessary discontent and jealousies when our very existence as a nation may depend on our union." Marshall declared that he would have opposed the Alien and Sedition laws in Congress, if he had been a member, and that he probably would have been able to prevent their enactment. He pledged, furthermore, to oppose their renewal if he was elected to Congress. He had already left Congress to become secretary of state, however, before renewal of the Alien and Sedition Acts was considered. Although Marshall led the struggle in the legislature against the Virginia Resolutions, James Madison's constitutional indictment of the Alien and Sedition Acts, this did not redeem him among Federalist leaders. Even young John Quincy Adams, who one day would describe Marshall as "one of the most eminent men that this country has ever produced," then viewed him as an apostate. "I suppose this is the way of putting the foot into the stirrup of oppositions," he said, and if Marshall goes to Congress, "we shall soon find him full mounted galloping with" the Jeffersonians. The most thorough damnation of Marshall came from that most bitter of Federalists, Fisher Ames of Massachusetts:

> No correct man,—no incorrect man even,—whose affections and feelings are wedded to the government, would give his name to the base opposers of law, as a means for its annoyance. This he has done. Excuses may palliate,—future zeal in the cause may partially atone,—but his character is done for. . . . Like a man who in battle receives an ounce ball in his body—it may heal, it lies too deep to be extracted; but, on every change of weather, it will be apt to fester and twinge. There let it lie. False federalists, or

such as act wrong from false fears, should be dealt hardly by, if I
were Jupiter Tonans. . . . The moderates are the meanest of cow-
ards, the falsest of hypocrites.*

Besides the unpardonable sin of moderation, the contemporary Federalist indictment of John Marshall contained three
articles, all of them ironic in light of his long career on the
bench. To the party leaders whose leadership he had ignored,
he was too democratic, too strict an interpreter of the Constitution, too Virginian.

Theodore Sedgwick, who was more understanding of Marshall's independence than most Federalists, described Marshall
as affectionate, honest, honorable, and immensely talented. His
"foolish declaration" on the Alien and Sedition Acts stemmed
not from malice but from his "strong attachment to
popularity."

> Hence it is that he is disposed on all popular subjects to feel the
> public pulse. . . . He is disposed to the erotic refinement, and to
> express great respect for the sovereign people, and to quote their
> opinions as an evidence of truth. The latter is of all things the
> most destructive of personal independence & of that weight of
> character which a great man ought to possess.†

George Cabot summed up Virginia Federalists succinctly as
"little better than half-way Jacobins" whose opinions would
never "prove sound according to New England ideas."

Oliver Wolcott, the High Federalist secretary of the treasury
who somehow eluded Adams' sweeping removals, saw Marshall
as "a man of virtue and distinguished talents" who "will think
much of the State of Virginia, and is too much disposed to
govern the world according to rules of logic; he will read and
expound the constitution as if it were a penal statute, and will

---

* Ames to Christopher Gore, December 18, 1798, in Seth Ames, ed.,
Works of Fisher Ames, 2 vols. (New York: William Gowans, 1869), vol. I,
p. 246.

† Sedgwick to Rufus King, May 11, 1800, in Charles R. King, ed., *The
Life and Correspondence of Rufus King,* 6 vols. (New York: G. P. Putnam's Sons, 1894–1900), vol. III, p. 237.

sometimes be embarrassed with doubts of which his friends will not perceive the importance."

Like New England historians of the nineteenth century, Marshall's fellow Federalists could never quite forgive him his birthplace. Those attempting to minimize his sin of party irregularity attributed it to the misfortune of his Virginia background. In 1799 George Cabot advised against Federalist attacks on Marshall because, once his enthusiasm was leavened with political experience, his able mind and charming disposition would make him "an accomplished political scholar and a very useful man." Allowance must be made, however, for "the influence of the atmosphere of Virginia, which doubtless makes everyone who breathes it visionary and, upon the subject of free government, incredibly credulous." Later that same year, Speaker Sedgwick admitted that Marshall was so widely respected among Southern Federalists that "we can do nothing without him." Yet, "I do believe he would have been a more decided man had his education been on the other side of the Delaware, and he the immediate representative of that country."

Naturally, a faction that could suspect John Adams of becoming a political ally of Thomas Jefferson, as many High Federalists predicted both in 1796 and 1800, would suspect the same of someone bearing the double taint of moderation and Virginia. James McHenry, the secretary of war whom Adams had attempted to replace with Marshall, passed on the rumor that "Mr. Marshall has signified that he does not mean to resign in the event of Mr. Jefferson being elected President, but to wait most patiently the development of his politics. Will there," McHenry concluded, "be so great an antipathy between the politics of the two gentlemen, that one of them must fly off from the other?" For McHenry, the obvious answer to his rhetorical question was "no." Oliver Wolcott, who knew John Marshall much better because of their service together in Adams' cabinet, replied that Marshall would certainly retire

in the event of Jefferson's election: "The opposition of sentiment between these men appears to be decided, and I believe
is unchangeable."

Compounding the pain of Marshall's appointment for many
Federalists was the fact that Marshall climbed over so obvious
a contender as Justice William Paterson. Senator James Hill-
house and Timothy Pickering of New England, James
McHenry of Maryland, and a host of lesser Federalist lumi-
naries happily assumed that Paterson was the only possible
choice if Jay refused to serve again. And Senator Jonathan
Dayton of Paterson's own state of New Jersey was positively
livid when Marshall was nominated. On the day of Marshall's
appointment, Dayton relayed the news to Paterson "with grief,
astonishment & almost indignation." Dayton was instrumental
in delaying action on the nomination for a week while seeking
means to reject Marshall or to persuade Adams to rescind his
nomination or Marshall his acceptance. He was fearful,
though, that if the Senate rejected Marshall, President Adams
would respond by nominating "some other character more
improper and more disgusting." To Dayton, the President's
appointments and conduct in the closing months of his administration "have manifested such debility or derangement of
intellect, that I am convinced, in common with the most of our
Federal members, that another four years of administration
in his hands would have exposed us to destruction."

After the Senate finally admitted defeat a week later and
confirmed Marshall's appointment, Dayton dispatched to
Paterson the consoling word that "all voices, with the exception of one only [President Adams], were united in favor of the
conferring of this appointment upon you." Consolation for
Dayton, himself, was his understanding that Marshall *"was not
privy to his own nomination, but had previously* exerted his
influence with the President" in Paterson's behalf. This is,
however, not entirely true. Although Marshall's autobiography
indicates that he had not sought or even dreamed of the posi-

tion of chief justice, he was at least informed of Adams' intention the day before the nomination, and he could have shaken his head, rather than nodded, if he were truly as eager as Dayton was for Paterson's advancement. Fortunately for Marshall, Paterson was a more gracious loser than his supporters, whom he, in turn, attempted to soothe. Paterson soon congratulated Marshall on his appointment, and their relationship on the bench for the next five years was cordial.

A "LAME-DUCK" APPOINTEE

In assaulting both President Adams and his nominee, the Federalists manifested what almost seemed to be a suicidal urge. The Jeffersonian Republicans, meanwhile, seemed indifferent to Marshall's appointment. Although they would soon attack Adams and the Federalists for "lame-duck" appointments to newly created offices, they seemed for the present to accept the appointment of a chief justice by a retiring President as one of the unfortunate rules of the game of politics.

In 1968 when Lyndon B. Johnson sought unsuccessfully to appoint Abe Fortas as chief justice, it would seem that he limped far less severely than John Adams in 1801. Johnson still had a half year to serve; he was leaving the White House semivoluntarily; and it was not even certain yet that the opposition party would assume the presidency. In 1968, however, there was a large and vocal coalition of Republican and Southern Democratic senators who could prevent, or at least delay, Fortas' confirmation. In 1801, by contrast, there were too few Jeffersonian Republicans in the Senate to influence the appointment. Thus they were content to let the Federalists squabble among themselves over which Federalist should be chief justice.

Surely the advancement of a personal enemy to lifetime tenure on the supreme bench rankled Thomas Jefferson, though for the moment even he remained silent. In January and February there was such concern over whether the Federalist House of Representatives would be able to make Aaron Burr President rather than Jefferson, that events in the Senate received less attention than they merited.

Republican and Federalist newspapers alike virtually ignored Marshall's assumption of office. Typical of newspapers throughout the country was Jefferson's pet journal in the District of Columbia, the *National Intelligencer,* which merely announced on January 21, "The President of the U.S. has nominated John Marshall Chief Justice of the United States." On February 4 it added, "The justices of the Supreme Court have made a Court—the following justices being present; viz. Messrs. Marshall, Cushing, Chase and Washington."

The shrill *Philadelphia Aurora* had scoffed that John Jay, "after having thro' decay of age become incompetent to discharge the duties of Governor, has been appointed to the *sinecure of Chief Justice* of the United States." Yet it viewed Marshall's appointment without rancor, perhaps because "sinecure" then seemed a fair description of the office. The *Aurora*'s sole concern seemed to be that Marshall should not be paid both as chief justice and as secretary of state; but the impropriety of even holding both offices for a month does not appear to have occurred to Editor William Duane. Perhaps it appealed to his Republican ideas of economy to have both offices filled for a single salary.

The one newspaper that really scorched Marshall was the *Richmond Examiner,* his own hometown newspaper. James T. Callender, a political pamphleteer who had fled England to escape conviction for sedition and who was currently sentenced to prison in the United States for the same offense, wrote in the issue of February 6, 1801, that "we are to have that precious acquisition, John Marshall, as Chief Justice. . . . The very sound of this man's name is an insult upon truth and justice." He contended, erroneously, that the appointment of Jay was only a front to hide Adams' intention to name Marshall when Jay refused, which Callender called a "previous certainty."

At the time, no one realized that Marshall's appointment was to become a major event in American history, which would be marked by centennial celebrations all across the country in 1901. Marshall had abilities, to be sure, but they did not seem to surpass those of John Jay or Oliver Ellsworth, William Paterson or Jared Ingersoll. The responsibility of guiding a new judiciary in a new system of government might be a great opportunity, but earlier members of the Supreme Court had not found it so. It remained to be seen whether or not John Marshall would employ his abilities to the maximum advantage of the opportunities presented. The fact that he was a Federalist in a lifetime office, at a time when Federalists were being driven from the executive and legislative branches and were, moreover, unwelcome in the judiciary, might increase his opportunities if he could assert the worthiest aspects of Federalism (most notably, nationalism) and avoid partisan wrangling with President Jefferson over the selfish and grubby aspects of Federalism.

◆§ 2 §◆

JOHN MARSHALL
FEDERALIST

———————◆◆◆———————

History records John Marshall as a political judge! Latter-day
Jeffersonians such as Claude G. Bowers cry shame as they
make the charge, while Federalist-leaning historians such as
Albert J. Beveridge give an indulgent wink to Marshall's
partisanship. No one really disputes the charge. There can be
no question that Marshall was a sincere Federalist; yet to say
(as Tom Watson, for instance, does) that Marshall was as
"rabid a partizan as ever lived" and that he would "fulminate
rank Federalism with authoritative voice for more than a
generation" is unjust. A High Federalist—an Alexander
Hamilton, Timothy Pickering, or Fisher Ames—would
probably have committed all the partisan offenses which are
generally charged against Marshall and would also probably
have been impeached because he lacked Marshall's instinct for
survival.

MARSHALL AND HAMILTON

The epithet "Federalist Judge" evokes a picture of Marshall that is harsher than justified. Because Alexander Hamilton—then and now—represents the epitome of Federalism, it is too often assumed that Marshall's Federalist decisions exude all the illiberal, proprietarian, and undemocratic airs of Hamiltonianism. Marshall's and Hamilton's ideas were similar in many respects, but his party leaders' suspicion of Marshall is compelling evidence that he was not a High Federalist. He did not rebel against party discipline because he was a mad or inexperienced Virginian, but because of an essential difference in political and social philosophy from the Northern wing of his party. He accepted most Federalist doctrine, but he always looked first to Washington, not Hamilton, for guidance; even Jefferson dared not openly condemn George Washington! John Quincy Adams and Joseph Story consciously distinguished between levels of Federalism when they described John Marshall as a "federalist of the Washington School."

Marshall was far more cautious and judicious (a worthwhile attribute in his new position) than the brilliant but passionate Hamilton. Hamilton's aristocratic ideas were not welcomed as enthusiastically by Marshall as they were by Hamilton's New England disciples. (Even Max Lerner, who portrayed Marshall in 1939 as a statesman almost solely motivated by his economic interests, had to admit Marshall was "no New England Brahman.") By the time he became chief justice, Marshall felt sheepish about his youthful enthusiasm for democracy, but the attitudes of his youth never entirely left him. Rather than shunning his rude frontier origins, as Hamilton sought to forget his West Indian poverty and bastardy, Marshall always maintained intimate social, if not political, ties with grass-roots Virginia. Even if Marshall's rural mannerisms may sometimes have been part of a role dictated by political opportunism, still it is obvious that it was a role for which he was well cast and which he immensely enjoyed. It is no accident that the same sort of apocryphal stories are told about John Marshall as about Abraham Lincoln. Marshall and Lincoln shared not only a similar method of reasoning, a reverence for the Union, and certain economic policies such as banking leadership by the federal government and government support of industry; they were likewise akin in their personalities and attitudes toward the people around them.

MARSHALL'S DRIVE FOR WEALTH

Although Marshall did not always *act* the part of a dutiful Federalist in Congress, he did share the economic ambitions which were so basic to the Hamiltonians. As a young lawyer practicing in the increasingly commercial town of Richmond in the 1780s and 1790s, Marshall's career was intimately tied with the litigious merchants who employed him. He speculated especially in lands and also in river improvement companies. By the time he was thirty-one he owned nearly a thousand acres of Virginia land.

His greatest venture into high finance came in 1793 when he, two relatives, and an old army comrade plunged far above their heads to purchase the remnant of the huge Fairfax estate, more than 160,000 acres in northern Virginia. The money for this immense speculation was borrowed from Robert Morris of Philadelphia, an early financial giant, whom Marshall had for some time represented in Virginia litigation. Marshall's links with the Morris empire were strengthened in 1795 when his brother James, a future federal judge himself, wed the sister of Robert Morris. James Madison, who was usually fairly tolerant of Marshall, remarked at the time of the Fairfax purchase that Marshall's "pecuniary aids from the Bank or people connected with it" must have made him feel "in the moment of purchase an absolute dependence on the monied interest, which will explain" his support for Federalist policies. Furthermore, Madison downgraded one young Virginian simply because the young man was friendly with Marshall.

Marshall's future was greatly influenced by this immense potential treasure and present burden. Whether or not he should accept political offices offered to him was determined in large part by their financial impact on the payment of his debt. He refused positions as attorney general, associate justice of the Supreme Court (in 1798), and secretary of war because they would pay less than his law practice. On the other hand, he accepted the commission to France—which, owing to Messrs. X, Y, and Z, made him a national political figure—because it would reward him handsomely for his time. He received $19,963.97, (including expenses which were surely less than $5,000) for an eleven-month mission. This exceeded the *combined* annual salaries of the associate justices of the United States Supreme Court. To help meet his financial burden, he also assumed a literary burden which plagued him for years; he undertook his massive *Life of Washington* because he thought the royalties would rescue his investment. Marshall may even have accepted appointment as chief justice, the office that lifted him—and that he, in turn, lifted—from minor status to that of a giant of American history, because he thought his leisure time on the bench would permit him to concentrate on his literary venture. Ironically, his judicial career completely dwarfs his meager contribution as an historian. In 1813 John Adams sneered at Marshall's *Washington* as a history written "to make money." It certainly did not earn for Marshall what he had anticipated, though he and Bushrod Washington do seem to have cleared about $18,500 each.

MODERATE FEDERALIST CONGRESSMAN

Marshall was accused of using his Federalist merchant friends to steal a seat in Congress in 1799. A resentful young constituent attributed Marshall's victory to "deceit and brib-ery." He alleged that the Scottish merchants' wealth, which was "gained by fraud and sunk in the deepest coffers of avarice, flowed with liberality in promoting the election of their favorite." As this condemnation of Marshall by a dis-appointed Republican was not picked up by the attentive Jefferson or his party lieutenants, it seems likely that Marshall was guilty only of "treating" the voters with liquid refresh-ment, a tradition in Virginia politics which was honored by Republicans and Federalists alike. Marshall felt that he, rather than the defeated John Clopton, was the injured party. He wrote his brother that the means used to defeat him "are despicable in the extreme and yet they succeed. Nothing I believe more debases or pollutes the human mind than faction."

Once in Congress Marshall demonstrated that his opposition to the Federalists' pet measures, the Alien and Sedition Acts, was not mere campaign oratory. He shocked his Federalist colleagues by voting to repeal the section of the Sedition Act that provided punishment for seditious speech. His faithful service in President John Adams' efforts to reestablish peace with France was regarded as a disservice by Federalist leaders in Congress; war with France was their assurance of tenure in office. Marshall's independence in opposing and eventually killing the Disputed Elections Bill only increased consterna-tion among the High Federalists. Rather than being "as rabid a partizan as ever lived," John Marshall was, in fact, remark-ably moderate—for a Federalist.

This moderation made him all the more formidable to the Jefferson administration. A more avid party man, a Samuel Chase, for instance, would have been sure to do something outlandish and suicidal; not so the cautious Marshall. From the moment he became chief justice, he remained remarkably clear of party politics. He was, of course, a skilled politician before he went on the bench; most successful Supreme Court justices have been. Nor did he shed his political principles and opinions when he donned the robes; few justices would be so self-disciplined (or so self-deceived) as to feel they have done this. Only a few hours before Jefferson's inauguration, Marshall wrote to Charles C. Pinckney that he was fully impressed with "the importance of the judiciary at all times but more especially the present" and that he would "endeavor in the new office to which I am called not to disappoint my friends." His party sword would remain sheathed, however, until it could be used with best effect. Marshall's political philosophy would frequently be asserted from the bench, never more notably than in the Marbury v. Madison, 1 Cranch 137 (1803), decision, but it was precisely because he shunned blatant partisanship that he succeeded in his more subtle playing of politics.

During Marshall's first month on the Supreme Court, the House of Representatives was locked in a titanic political struggle over the presidency. Republican representatives fought to overcome the effects of a careless tie vote in the electoral college that was permitting a Federalist-dominated House to determine which Republican would become President, Thomas Jefferson or Aaron Burr. Federalists worked equally hard to hurt Jefferson by awarding the office to his ostensible vice-presidential candidate, Aaron Burr. Through it all, Marshall remained officially aloof. Although, privately, he leaned toward Burr, he refused to intervene publicly for either candidate. In later years Marshall's recollection was that he had not even voted in a presidential election "since the establishment of the general ticket system." By this he must have meant either the establishment of the bloc electoral ticket in Virginia in 1800 or the ratification of the Twelfth Amendment in 1804. In either case, he must have been wrong. It is inconceivable that Marshall resisted one or both opportunities to vote against his old foe Thomas Jefferson and for his old friends John Adams and Charles C. Pinckney. More likely his abstention from the polls began in 1808, the year in which the more tolerable James Madison was elected.

Although he disliked and distrusted Jefferson and his policies, Marshall remained remarkably silent on matters of public affairs throughout the Jefferson administrations. To be sure, he lectured the President in 1803 (*Marbury* v. *Madison*), and he subpoenaed him in 1807 (*United States* v. *Aaron Burr*).* Nevertheless, to view these two events as an unceasing eight-year judicial war against the executive is as false as to contend (as is too often done) that because President Jefferson stretched the Constitution in order to purchase Louisiana in 1803 and embargo American shipping in 1807 he was a traitor to Jefferson ideals.

NONPARTISANSHIP

Nonpartisanship came more easily to Marshall during the happier years between the administrations of Thomas Jefferson and Andrew Jackson. He was impressed by "the superior talents of Mr. Madison" in 1808, for instance, even though he was distressed by Madison's "inveterate & incurable" prejudices against Great Britain. Marshall's principal fear about Madison was that the latter would continue the policies of Jefferson. If he did, Marshall thought the nation would be in an unparalleled state of peril. "The internal changes which have been already made & those further changes which are contemplated by a party always hostile to our Constitution & which has for some time ruled our country despotically, must give serious alarm to every attentive & intelligent observer." Yet these domestic perils were minor when compared with those which would result from a pro-French foreign policy which threatened to make American independence "an empty name."

---

* *Annals of Congress*, 10th Cong., 1st sess., 385–778.

Despite his fears, Marshall resolved to stay out of active politics and devote any spare time "to agricultural pursuits." He would only "look on with silent & anxious concern," for there was nothing he could do about the low state of American politics. Because he cultivated his own garden, Marshall maintained good relations with the executive—Presidents James Madison, James Monroe, and John Quincy Adams—for the next two decades. He felt "excessive mortification" when Madison's foreign policy involved the United States in the War of 1812, but even then he would "indulge these feelings" only in private. He sought to avoid "those questions which agitate & excite the feelings of party" during "Mr. Madison's War."

Marshall probably hoped to continue this amicable relationship even beyond 1828. Although he privately favored Adams' candidacy against Andrew Jackson, he deeply resented the attempts of Whig journals to inject him into the political campaign that year. He protested the attribution to him of "intemperate language" which "does not become my age or office, and is foreign from my disposition and habits." After a few years of Jacksonian democracy, however, the aged judge was less circumspect and became an open and active leader of Virginia Whigs. Even in the Virginia constitutional convention of 1829, Marshall permitted a glimpse of the political man still underlying the judicial robes after nearly three decades of judicial restraint. A perceptive observer remarked that "the venerable judge is somewhat alive to those passions which we might be apt to imagine his elevated station, established fame, and above all, his great age, had lulled to perpetual repose in his bosom."

SECRETARY MARSHALL AT MIDNIGHT

Marshall's judicial career was remarkably nonpartisan overall, especially when compared with his first month as chief justice. During that brief period when his judicial* career overlapped the conclusion of his political life, his judicial robes received political stains that were not easily removed or forgotten. Justice Marshall could not control Secretary of State Marshall. Unfortunately, at the time when executive and judiciary coincided in the person of John Marshall, diplomacy was set aside and the secretary of state's duties were primarily politics and patronage. The two key figures in the flurry of activity surrounding the manning of scores of new offices, plus as many old ones as possible, were President Adams and Secretary Marshall.

Besides the mere paper work of consummating last-month and last-minute appointments, Secretary Marshall was also the major intermediary between the President and persons who wished to nominate "deserving" Federalists for office or who professed to be "deserving" partisans themselves. Marshall handled the completion of one appointment so badly that he virtually created the *Marbury* v. *Madison* case, but, when one considers the political credentials of those who became federal officeholders, it is clear that Marshall and Adams were not careless about whom they appointed. Senator Humphrey Marshall of Kentucky used unconscious irony when he wrote his cousin John Marshall in February 1801 to suggest a "deserving" (and rare in Kentucky) "friend to the Government" as circuit judge. If the secretary could "conceive that political opinions often have an influence in decisions upon private rights," he would realize the importance of placing on the bench "a man well affected to the federal Government," to counterbalance Republican enemies to the Constitution. This conception was well within John Marshall's and John Adams' capacity, so the Kentucky Federalist, William McClung, received the appointment. The flood of appointments of Federalists to office in Adams' last weeks in Washington was Jefferson's principal complaint against his predecessor. Marshall played an important role in the Midnight Appointments, so he was an important sharer in the blame. There was much partisan activity for the Jeffersonians to forgive during Marshall's first month as chief justice, and Jefferson and his followers were *not* in a forgiving mood.

Even despite his Midnight activities, Marshall was a paragon of propriety compared with some other judges of the day. Whereas Marshall served for a month as both chief justice and secretary of state, John Jay was chief justice and acting secretary of state for six months while President Washington awaited Jefferson's return from France and his decision whether to become Secretary of State. Jay ran unsuccessfully for governor of New York while still on the Supreme Court, and he even held the judicial office for more than a year while on a mission to England, where he negotiated the treaty that became the major political issue of the early 1790s. Oliver Ellsworth was chief justice *in absentia* for a year and a half, immediately before Marshall's appointment, while on a commission to negotiate peace with France.

Justices Bushrod Washington and Samuel Chase campaigned actively for the Federalist ticket in 1800, Chase even forsaking meetings of the Supreme Court to mount the political rostrum. William Paterson was more circumspect, though this did not prevent him from delivering "a most elegant and appropriate charge" to a jury in May 1800, in which he described "the Jacobins as the disorganizers of our happy country, and the only instruments of introducing discontent and dissatisfaction among the well meaning part of the community."

Unjudicious partisanship extended to state courts and Republican judges as well. Chancellor Robert R. Livingston of New York and Chief Justice Thomas McKean of Pennsylvania, both Republicans, had campaigned actively for Jefferson as President. Chief Justice Francis Dana of Massachusetts countered by describing Jefferson to the grand jury as an apostle of "atheism and anarchy, bloodshed and plunder."

Three members of the New Hampshire Supreme Court even went so far as to serve as presidential electors. Although it, too, was politically motivated, there was justice in Charles Pinckney's question whether a man brought before such judges could receive a fair trial, "particularly if his expressions have been levelled at the candidate those Judges have been electioneering to support." When Federalists in Congress gave the following toast on the eve of the first session of the Marshall Court, "The judiciary of the United States—independent of party, independent of power, and independent of popularity," they must have silently inserted the adjective, "Jefferson's," before the words "party," "power," and "popularity."

With such unjudicious and uncourtly behavior in recent memory, it was certain that the Jeffersonians in control of the legislative and executive branches of government would prepare for a struggle with the Federalist-dominated judiciary. Without this conflict the *Marbury* v. *Madison* case would have been meaningless if, indeed, it had occurred at all. Absent-mindedly, almost accidentally, John Adams had provided the judiciary with a leader who was worthy of Jefferson's thrusts and, perhaps, capable of withstanding them.

⤳ 3 ⤦

MARSHALL VERSUS JEFFERSON

———————◆———————

There were Federalists whose appointment would have upset Jefferson more than John Marshall's—but not many. Alexander Hamilton, who had declined the appointment as chief justice when it was offered to him by Washington in 1796, surely would have been harder for Jefferson to accept. Probably one of the more virulent New England Federalists such as Fisher Ames or Timothy Pickering would also have been more offensive to Jefferson than Marshall. Marshall's Federalism was, after all, mild, his conduct exemplary, and his language gentle, when compared with Hamilton, Ames, or Pickering. Among Federalists of national reputation, it would have been difficult to find one more likely to reach a workable relationship with the Jeffersonians than John Marshall— except for one problem. John Marshall and Thomas Jefferson despised each other.

YOUNG VIRGINIANS

Marshall and Jefferson had so much in common that one might expect them to be comrades rather than personal enemies. They were third cousins, once removed, descending, as did so many notable Virginians, from William Randolph of Turkey Island. Jefferson had his troubles with some other relatives, especially John Randolph of Roanoke. Marshall's family history, on the other hand, with the marked exception of Thomas Jefferson, was one of cherishing and caring for family members. Jeffersonians charged that Secretary of State Marshall provided *too* well for his brothers and cousins, providing too many of them with federal offices. Marshall even remained on friendly personal terms with his cousin John Randolph, a difficult feat for anyone but especially so for someone who differed so completely from Randolph in politics.

Jefferson and Marshall were born—a half-generation apart —near the frontier, far enough east to remain essentially Virginians, yet far enough west to be vitally influenced by the frontier. Their homelife, and especially their relationship with their down-to-earth fathers, was remarkably similar. At their fathers' urging, they determined early on law as a career, and both studied under the same great teacher, though Jefferson's contact with George Wythe was long and intimate, whereas Marshall's was brief and distant. (Jefferson as a legislator had revolutionized the curriculum at the College of William and Mary, making it possible for Marshall to learn a good deal about law in a mere six months.) In August 1780 Governor Jefferson, probably without forebodings of trials to come, licensed John Marshall to practice before the Virginia bar. Their legal careers were interrupted by the American Revolution, in which both served well, though at vastly different levels, as would be expected from the twelve-year difference in their ages.

Yet, in the words of the great Jeffersonian scholar Julian Boyd, "out of this remarkable identity of background came one of the mighty opposites of American history." The origin of this lifelong enmity is not known. By the time Marshall and Jefferson began speaking of each other in surviving correspondence, a strain was already evident, but the letters do not explain why. Assuming that the antagonism was not congenital, perhaps the American Revolution itself diverted them into such different, yet conflicting, paths. Marshall's service was entirely military. Unlike General Washington, whose responsibilities were political and diplomatic as well as military, Captain Marshall saw only the failures of civil authorities, never the difficulties they met and occasionally surmounted. Possibly his cousin Thomas, whose career Marshall would probably have followed closely because of their relationship, became the symbol to this young officer of the failure of American states and statesmen to provide adequately for their defenders.

Marshall always regarded the "suffering winter" of 1777–1778 at Valley Forge as the key to his nationalist philosophy. While Marshall was at Valley Forge, Jefferson served in the Virginia House of Delegates and necessarily bore some of the blame for what Washington and his army regarded as inexcusable neglect by Congress and the states.

The tables were turned with unjustified vengeance in 1781, when there was no army to aid Governor Jefferson's fruitless efforts to repel an overwhelming British force under Lord Cornwallis. British General Banastre Tarleton's determination to capture the Governor and his colleagues gave Jefferson no option but to run. The need and speed of his departure were so impressive that the fleeing Governor became the butt of frequent jokes to the likewise ambulatory Amblers, a family into which John Marshall would soon marry. Jacquelin Ambler, who was on the Council of State when Jefferson was governor and who later served with great distinction as treasurer of Virginia, remained on friendly terms with Jefferson. However, Ambler's wife, Rebecca, may still have resented the youthful romance which Jefferson had permitted to wither in 1763. He had ardently wooed Rebecca Burwell, but he stopped short lest marriage hinder his studies and travels. When Jefferson invited her to wait his return from Europe, she was not overwhelmed by the honor of having her name borne to many lands by a quixotic lover sailing the *Rebecca*. She chose, instead, to change her name to Ambler. The hilarity with which Rebecca's daughters—among them, John Marshall's fiancee—related Jefferson's misadventures in 1781 shows that he was an unheroic, if not comic, figure to the Ambler family. The girls probably knew that Jefferson *might* have been their father and were glad he was not. In part, then, Marshall may have *married* into his antagonism for Thomas Jefferson.

POLITICAL PHILOSOPHIES

Whatever lay at the roots of this historic unfriendship, each gave the other ample cause to nurture it during the coming decades. A conflict that may only have been personal to begin with became political during the 1790s, when Thomas Jefferson helped guide the party opposing the policies of Marshall's lifelong idol, George Washington. Perhaps Marshall himself best summed up his relationship with Jefferson when he remarked in an extremely bitter letter, four years after Jefferson's death, that "those Virginians who opposed the opinions and political views of Mr. Jefferson seem to have been considered rather as rebellious subjects than legitimate enemies entitled to the rights of political war."

From 1801 to 1809, as President Jefferson and Chief Justice Marshall glared at each other across the mud or dust of Washington, D.C., philosophical differences were added to their personal and political differences. Marshall stood philosophically between Thomas Jefferson and Alexander Hamilton, the two political giants of the era, though he was closer to the latter. Hamilton's views of the judiciary as interpreter of the Constitution and of broad construction of the Constitution were especially powerful influences on Marshall. He leaned heavily on Hamilton's *Federalist No. 78* in his advocacy of judicial interpretation in *Marbury* v. *Madison*. He was similarly influenced by Hamilton's broad construction arguments on the First National Bank in McCulloch v. Maryland, 4 Wheaton 316 (1819). This decision provided a historic blend of broad construction and judicial interpretation. Marshall, though, never worshiped the "rich and well-born" in the manner of Hamilton and his High Federalist disciples. Even when he was delivering Supreme Court decisions which would protect the property of wealthy speculators (like himself), there is no evidence that Marshall advocated a permanent and self-perpetuating aristocracy such as that desired by Hamilton. The property that Marshall regarded as most deserving of protection was that which was earned by the owner, rather than inherited wealth.

Marshall was far from High Federalism, but he was farther yet from Jeffersonian Republicanism. The disparity between Marshall's and Jefferson's concept of mankind is ably summed up in Robert K. Faulkner's remark that "Jefferson's doctrine of man's natural rights was more benevolent, yielded more discretion to individual choice, concerned itself less with protecting those who accumulated wealth and power and more with directly relieving suffering, especially through the modern useful sciences." Jefferson's concern for the well-being of the common man made him more fearful of the inequities which would result from the growth of a commercial-industrial America; Marshall's decisions, on the other hand, contributed significantly to the economic development which Jefferson feared.

Yet the difference between Jefferson and Marshall was one of degree—and the angle was much less than 180 degrees.

Marshall, like Jefferson, was a lifelong believer in natural rights and, therefore, limited government. He resented the extent to which these basic American ideals had come to be regarded as solely Jeffersonian. When a young acquaintance wrote in 1830 that Jefferson's ideas were most conducive to society's freedom and happiness, Marshall demanded to know the basis of such a view. It could not be based on Jefferson's opinion that "all political power originally resides in and must be derived from the people by their free consent, and ought to be exercised for their happiness," nor on his view that "rulers are accountable to the people for their conduct." This philosophy is "common to all the people and statesmen of America. Mr. Jefferson's opinions on these subjects, though 'in accordance with the freedom and happiness of society' are not more so than 'have been given to the world' by every patriot of The United States." He insisted that Jefferson's alleged preeminence must be based on "something peculiar to himself—not professed in common with all his country men." Marshall suggested that the automatic expiration of contracts and constitutions after a generation, the desirability of inter-mittent revolutions, elective judges and juries, periodical amendments, and so forth, were ideas which were, indeed, *peculiar* and therefore more properly Jeffersonian. Marshall's unwillingness to abandon natural rights advocacy to the Jeffersonians indicates that his philosophical differences with Jefferson were not as fundamental as they have sometimes appeared. Both were tremendously influenced by liberal English philosophers such as John Locke and David Hume.

On the key political issues of federalism and republicanism their differences were also ones of degree. Jefferson has come down in history as the fountainhead of state rights, Marshall as a giant of nationalism. Yet neither opposed federalism, they merely interpreted it differently. Jefferson did not want to destroy the central government, nor did Marshall seek to destroy the states. Each sought to maintain the proper balance within the federal system as he saw it, but, whereas Jefferson regarded centralization as the principal threat, Marshall regarded fragmentation as the principal threat. Both were firm believers in republican government, yet each saw the other as a threat to representative government. Jefferson seemed to Marshall to be leading an uneducated rabble to political dominance; Marshall was regarded by Jefferson as an advocate of monarchy or, at least, aristocracy. Each view is equally unfair.

After the election of Jefferson, Marshall could never feel as confident of popular rule as he did in his "wild and enthusiastic" youth. He was increasingly critical of democracy after 1800. Although he could respect an electorate which twice chose George Washington unanimously as President, Marshall was disheartened by an electorate which twice chose the leader of the opposition to Washington's policies, Thomas Jefferson.

Unfortunately, it is difficult—if not impossible—to find in Marshall's writings a comprehensive political theory which would place him precisely on the political spectrum between Jefferson and Hamilton. Marshall lives primarily through his decisions, because he was careless in the preservation—and sometimes careful in the destruction—of his private papers. He was not bound as closely as most judges by the limits of the case before him, but the judicial setting did not give him the same opportunities for political speculation as an untiring correspondent and pamphleteer such as Thomas Jefferson. It must also be added that Marshall was far less prone to deep political speculation than Jefferson. If Marshall's comprehensive political philosophy could be determined, it would probably be close to the conservative—yet moderate—philosophy of John Adams. Adams is regarded today as the American forefather of constructive conservatism. In his own day, however, he was practically drummed out of his own party because of his moderation. Adams was even suspected by the High Federalist (or Hamiltonian) leaders of flirting with the Jeffersonians. Marshall's position was lower, so the High Federalists' dudgeon was correspondingly lower. By the time that Marshall became a worthier target, after 1801, the High Federalists had so dwindled in influence that their opinion of Marshall or Adams no longer mattered.

POLITICAL AND PERSONAL ENEMIES

Jefferson correctly assessed Marshall as a potential opponent as early as 1792, when the thirty-seven-year-old Virginian was first proposed as a member of Congress. That it was Treasury Secretary Hamilton, already *the* enemy of Secretary of State Jefferson, who recommended Marshall must have increased Jefferson's concern. Jefferson tipped off Madison that Hamilton had "expressed the strongest desire that Marshall should come into Congress from Richmond, declaring that there is no man in Virginia whom he so much wishes to see there, and I am told that Marshall has expressed half a mind to come." Jefferson concluded from this interest in Marshall that Hamilton had "plyed him well with flattery and sollicitation, and I think nothing better could be done than to make him a judge." What better proof could there be of the lack of stature of the judiciary prior to Marshall's struggle for judicial power?

Regarding that same period, Marshall wrote in 1830:

> In truth, I have been a skeptic on this subject from the time I became acquainted with Mr. Jefferson as Secretary of State. I have never believed firmly in his infallibility. I have never thought him a particularly wise sound and practical statesman; nor have I ever thought those opinions which were peculiar to himself "most in accordinance [sic] with the freedom and happiness of society that have ever been given to the world." I have not changed this mode of thinking.*

It was in this same letter that he remarked that Virginians who thought as Marshall did were regarded as "rebellious subjects."

---

* Marshall to Henry Lee, October 25, 1830, Accession #5589, University of Virginia Library.

In 1795 Jefferson professed to welcome Marshall's election to the Virginia General Assembly, because he anticipated that it would force Marshall to show his true Federalist colors. Marshall had already distinguished himself as practically the only Virginian besides Washington who dared to defend the Jay Treaty with England. While Marshall might "embarras the Republican party in the assembly a good deal, yet upon the whole, his having gone into it will be of service." Clearly Marshall's plebeian mannerisms rankled Jefferson, who grumbled:

> He has been hitherto able to do more mischief acting under the mask of republicanism than he will be able to do after throwing it plainly off. His lax lounging manners have made him popular with the bulk of the people of Richmond and a profound hypocrisy [has made him popular] with many thinking men in our country. but having come forth in the plenitude of his English principles [by supporting the Jay Treaty] the latter will see that it is high time to make him known.*

Ironically, President Jefferson tried to demonstrate the extent of his "Revolution of 1800" by affecting some of the same "lax lounging manners" which came so naturally to John Marshall. New England Federalists and their Old England associates were appalled by the President's abandonment of the trappings and ceremonies of authority, but there is no evidence that Marshall disapproved. Perhaps he thought that Jefferson was finally acting the way a gentleman from western Virginia, especially one who professed to be a great democrat, should act.

Jefferson's suspicion of Marshall's "English principles" was heartily reciprocated by Marshall's fear of Jefferson's Francophilia. Marshall was quite public in his expressions of concern over the "overweening partiallity for France" which Jefferson had "unfortunately imbibed" on his mission there. He feared

---

* Jefferson to Madison, November 26, 1795, Library of Congress: Jefferson Papers.

that if Jefferson became President, this love for France would be "the fruitful source of woe to our country." When Jefferson learned of Marshall's remarks, he abruptly halted the very limited and very strained social contacts which he had previously had with his congressman cousin. Later, when Jefferson was elected, Marshall protested that his "foreign prejudices seem to me totally to unfit him for the chief magistracy."

Despite their widely differing views regarding France and England, Jefferson still had some hope for Marshall's redemption when Marshall first returned from his diplomatic mission to France in 1798. Even though Jefferson was sure that Marshall had been pumped with "more than hints from Hamilton as to the tone required to be assumed" in his report, he felt that Marshall was "not hot enough," or anti-French enough, to suit the Federalists. Edward Livingston, a Republican, was the source of Jefferson's optimism regarding Marshall's likely response to his treatment in France. Jefferson, for instance, complained that Federalist rumors were "diametrically opposite to what [Marshall] said to Livingston"—or at least to what Livingston *said* he said. The Vice-President was so concerned about what Marshall might report about France that he attempted to pay him a personal visit at his Philadelphia inn. Marshall was absent, so Jefferson left a note expressing "that respect which in company with his fellow citizens he bears him." In this third-person note, Jefferson made a fascinating slip which can only be regarded as Freudian: "He had the honor of calling at [Marshall's] lodgings twice this morning," wrote Jefferson, "but was so lucky as to find that he was out on both occasions." Upon rereading the note, Jefferson corrected it by inserting "un" before "lucky." Years later, Marshall chuckled that for once Jefferson came pretty close to telling the truth. Jefferson did not long remain in doubt regarding Marshall's report and its political impact. After the Republicans in Congress foolishly coerced President Adams

into publicizing the report, Jefferson bemoaned the "wicked use . . . made of the French negociation; and particularly of the XYZ dish cooked up by Marshall where the swindlers are made to appear as the French government."

THE ELECTION OF 1800

Even if Jefferson and Marshall had somehow been friends prior to the election of 1800 and the electoral crisis of 1801, their friendship could not have survived the strains of the hot political winter of 1800–1801. It is likely that Representative Marshall made possible the election of Jefferson by his morally responsible but politically dangerous opposition to the Disputed Elections Bill in April and May of 1800, but Marshall won no praise from Jefferson. This bill, as it came from the Senate, would have made Federalist leaders in Congress the final judge of disputes regarding presidential electors. Marshall's insistence on amendments killed the entire measure. Jefferson's victory was only a regrettable aftereffect of Marshall's action, and the Federalists had not, of course, been so brazen (or honest) as to label their measure the "Beat Jefferson Bill." Thus Jefferson need not have specifically thanked Marshall, though he should certainly have been thankful that Congress rejected the Disputed Elections Bill. Ever suspicious of Marshall, Jefferson grumbled instead about the deviousness of the very amendments that led to the destruction of this bill and Adams' chances for reelection. Marshall knew his opponents well enough to predict that whatever he did "the democrats will abuse me & therefore I need only to satisfy myself." At that same time Jefferson was urging Governor Monroe that "nothing should be spared to eradicate" the "federalism & Marshalism" which infested Richmond. Edmund Randolph had written in 1797 that Marshall and his political associates had converted Richmond into "little more than a colony of Philadelphia."

Marshall's confidence that Adams would be elected anyway may have helped him make the decision for political honesty rather than expediency when he opposed the Disputed Elections Bill. He happily reported in March 1800 that the odds were "more than two to one" in Adams' favor. Then why taint certain victory with dirty politics? The outlook, however, soon changed drastically. By August Marshall detected a powerful current against his party. "There is a tide in the affairs of nations, of parties, and of individuals," he said. "I fear that of real Americanism is on the ebb." By real Americanism he meant, of course, Washington-Adams Federalism. By October he was trying to buoy up Federalists against the deluge. He urged District Judge Richard Peters of Pennsylvania, for instance, to remember that "However the election may terminate good men ought still to continue their endeavors for the public happiness. I pray devoutly (which is no very common practice with me) that the future administration may do as little harm as the present & the past." By December 1800 the dejected Marshall could write that as he had "no voice in the election, & in fact scarcely any wish concerning it, I do not intermeddle with it." The only question remaining then was which *Republican* would be President, Thomas Jefferson or his running mate, Aaron Burr, who through sloppy party management had received an equal number of electoral votes.

Marshall was more concerned about the Jefferson-Burr runoff than his comment would imply. Unlike Alexander Hamilton and Gouverneur Morris, Federalist leaders who exerted themselves to have the House of Representatives break the tie in Jefferson's favor, Marshall (like most other Federalists) preferred Burr as the lesser of evils. Hamilton despised and feared Aaron Burr, his longtime competitor from New York City. Marshall, on the other hand, scarcely knew Burr and so was influenced largely by his personal distaste for fellow-Virginian Jefferson. Senator Morris of New York was more responsible than either Hamilton or Marshall, when he "greatly disapproved, and openly disapproved" the Federalist attempt to advance Burr over Jefferson. Instead of being moved by personal animus, as were Hamilton and Marshall, Morris merely felt that "since it was evidently the intention of our fellow citizens to make Mr. Jefferson their President, it seems proper to fulfil that intention." Even so caustic a critic of democracy as Gouverneur Morris could clearly see that the American people had spoken for Jefferson, and he opposed taking advantage of a faulty electoral system to subvert that decision.

Marshall could not be persuaded to work for Jefferson, but at least he pledged not to work against him. There is no evidence, however, that Marshall would have become involved in the Jefferson-Burr embroglio anyway. Marshall's answer to Hamilton's entreaties on January 1, 1801, sums up a decade or more of antagonism and suspicion of Thomas Jefferson:

> Being no longer in the house of representatives, & consequently compeled by no duty to decide between them, my own mind had scarcely determind to which of these gentlemen the preference was due. To Mr. Jefferson, whose political character is better known than that of Mr. Burr, I have felt almost insuperable objections. His foreign prejudices seem to me totally to unfit him for the chief magistracy of a nation which can not indulge those prejudices without sustaining deep & permanent injury. In addition to this solid & immoveable objection Mr. Jefferson appears to me to be a man who will embody himself with the house of representatives. By weakening the office of President he will increase his personal power. He will diminish his responsibility, sap the fundamental principles of the government & become the leader of that party which is about to constitute the majority of the legislature. The morals of the author of the letter to Mazzei cannot be pure.
>
> With these impressions concerning Mr. Jefferson, I was in some degree disposed to view with less apprehension any other character, & to consider the alternative now offerd as a circumstance not to be entirely neglected.
>
> Your representation of Mr. Burr with whom I am totally unacquainted shows that from him still greater danger than even from Mr. Jefferson may be apprehended. Such a man as you describe is

more to be feared, and may do more immediate if not greater mischief. Believing that you know him well & are impartial my preference woud certainly not be for him—but I can take no part in this business. I cannot bring myself to aid Mr. Jefferson. Perhaps respect for myself shoud, in my present situation, deter me from using any influence (if indeed I possessd any) in support of either gentleman. Altho no consideration coud induce me to be the secretary of state while there was a President whose political system I believd to be at variance with my own, yet this cannot be so well known to others, & it might be suspected that a desire to be well with the successful candidate had in some degree governd my conduct.*

Marshall expressed similar views to other correspondents. Three days earlier, he had written Edward Carrington of Virginia that the decision between Burr and Jefferson was "a choice of evils & I really am uncertain which woud be the greatest." He added, though, that it was not believed that Burr "would weaken the vital parts of the constitution, nor is it believed that he has any undue foreign attachments." Jefferson was, of course, presumed guilty on both counts. Marshall wrote Rufus King, the Federalist who was Adams' minister to Great Britain and who would for some time continue as Jefferson's representative at the Court of St. James, to predict that Jefferson would seek "to strengthen the state governments at the expense of that of the Union & to transfer as much as possible the powers remaining with the general government to the floor of the house of representatives."

Jefferson could not know of Marshall's private speculation regarding Jeffersonianism and Burrism, but two more public events in January 1801 sufficed to earn for Marshall Jefferson's undying resentment. Most important, of course, was Marshall's appointment as chief justice at the end of the month, depriving Jefferson of a nomination which in six weeks would have been his to make. More immediately alarming, however, was

* Marshall to Hamilton, January 1, 1801, Library of Congress: Hamilton Papers.

an alleged plot, rumored early in January, to deprive both Burr and Jefferson of the presidency and bestow it upon—of *all* people—John Marshall. As early as January 6, 1801, Governor James Monroe of Virginia had scented hints of a Federalist plot to "commit the power by a Legislative act to John Marshall, Samuel A. Otis, or some other person till another election," if the House of Representatives was unable to decide between Burr and Jefferson. As Otis was only secretary of the Senate, an office he held from 1789 to 1814, Secretary of State Marshall was the more formidable threat to Jefferson. On January 10 the *Philadelphia Aurora* publicized the supposed conspiracy to make Marshall President. By January 18 Monroe had word, probably from Representative John Randolph, that "Marshall has given an opinion in conversation with" Secretary of the Navy Benjamin Stoddert that "in case 9 States should not unite in favor of one of the persons chosen, the Legislature may appoint a President till another election is made, and that intrigues are carrying to place us in that situation." (Ironically, it was Stoddert who managed an abortive campaign in 1812 to win the Federalist nomination for Marshall as the peace candidate against the more hawkish James Madison.) In 1801 Governor Monroe emphasized that the state of Virginia would use force, if necessary, to unseat "President Marshall," Virginian or not.

Monroe's suspicions of Marshall may have been justified, for the *Washington Federalist* of January 6, 1801, carried an article asserting Congress' authority to provide for a vacancy if the President could not be chosen "in the manner prescribed by the constitution." Marshall's biographer, Albert J. Beveridge, contends that the article is "so perfectly in Marshall's method of reasoning and peculiar style of expression that his authorship would appear to be reasonably certain." Furthermore, Marshall's ties with this Federalist newspaper were so intimate that it would not have been surprising to find him writing for it. Therefore, whether or not Marshall was actually involved in a plot to deprive Thomas Jefferson of the presidency, Jefferson could not help *suspecting* that he was.

CHIEF JUSTICE VERSUS PRESIDENT

Despite plots, suspicions, and accusations, the two antagonists made a show of the proper amenities when Marshall, in one of his first acts as chief justice, administered the oath of office at President Jefferson's inauguration. Thus Marshall and Jefferson were the central figures in the dramatic ceremony which marked the transfer of power from dying Federalism to Republicanism. On March 2 Jefferson asked the chief justice to meet him two days later at the Capitol to administer the oath of office. He also asked Marshall to accept a one-day "reappointment" as secretary of state to countersign some documents. Ironically, Jefferson began their new relationship in new offices by asking Marshall's advice on a question verging on the review of legislation. "I would pray you in the meantime to consider whether the oath prescribed in the Constitution be not the only one necessary to take?" he urged. That oath seemed to Jefferson to "comprehend the substance of that prescribed by the Act of Congress to all officers, and it may be questionable whether the Legislature can require any new oath from the President." Marshall and Jefferson agreed at least on this first constitutional question, and the longer oath required of other government officials was bypassed. Four years later, when the same protagonists met again for the same ceremony, the *Philadelphia Aurora* complained that "the Judge" had turned "his back upon the President whilst administering the oath" in 1801. As Jefferson left no record of such a slight, it seems likely that Editor William Duane's active imagination was playing tricks on his memory.

Actually, Marshall felt somewhat better after the dreaded inauguration than he had earlier. On the morning of March

4, he wrote the defeated Federalist vice-presidential candidate, Charles C. Pinckney, of his wish

> . . . that the public prosperity & happiness may sustain no diminution under democratic guidance. The democrats are divided into speculative theorists & absolute terrorists. With the latter I am not disposd to class Mr. Jefferson. If he arranges himself with them it is not difficult to foresee that much calamity is in store for our country.

At 4 P.M. that same day he added:

> I have administerd the oath to the President. You will before this reaches you see his inauguration speech. It is in the general well judgd & conciliatory. It is in direct terms giving the lie to the violent party declamation which has elected him, but it is strongly characteristic of the general cast of his political theory.*

By the end of the year, each protagonist was in more characteristic form. The wife of Justice William Cushing reported confidentially to Mrs. John Adams that "the CJ" thought that Jefferson's first annual message to Congress "reduced the strength of the Government to the old Confederation."

Warm friendships have been significant in American political and constitutional history. The close companionship of Thomas Jefferson and James Madison, for instance, vitally affected the development of the American party system. The remarkable teamwork and friendship of John Marshall and Joseph Story left an important imprint on the development of the United States Supreme Court and, hence, the United States Constitution. So, too, have heated enmities been significant. Without the political and personal antagonism of Thomas Jefferson and John Marshall the *Marbury* v. *Madison* decision could not have been the same. Without that decision as at least a small foot-in-the-doorway to judicial power, American constitutional history might very well have been modified. To

---

* Marshall to Pinckney, March 4, 1801, Charleston Library Society, Charleston, S. C.

be sure, there were halting steps toward a limited judicial review prior to the *Marbury* decision, but as yet the Supreme Court had not clearly asserted the doctrine. If the judges of the late nineteenth century had to rely solely on the disastrously unpopular *Dred Scott* decision (Dred Scott v. Sandford, 19 Howard 393 [1857]) as a precedent for invalidating federal legislation, rather than on the *Marbury* decision by "the Great Chief Justice," they might have been much more timid in their exercise of judicial review.

HISTORIANS CONTINUE THE CONFLICT

There is a danger of overemphasizing the impact of the antagonism between Jefferson and Marshall—but to ignore it would likewise distort history. Historians have most often erred on the side of overemphasis—with a sizable admixture of political bias. Too often the historian's own politics can be determined by whether he blames the conflict on Marshall or Jefferson. The tone of John Quincy Adams' assessment of the "crafty and quixotic" Jefferson dominated historical accounts of the Marshall-Jefferson relationship for a century. The giant of Marshall biographers, Albert J. Beveridge, regretted his "thorough study of Jefferson" because it "has disillusioned me concerning that commanding figure in our history." Although Senator Beveridge was well acquainted with twentieth-century demagogues, he doubted that there was "an example in the history of our own or any other country of so shifty a politician and so reckless a demagogue as Jefferson." Beveridge was at least concerned about his assumption that whereas Marshall was too honest to engage in a personal vendetta, for Jefferson "a personal antagonism, once formed, became . . . a public policy."

Another history-writing senator, Henry Cabot Lodge, reveled in the detection of the "feline hostility of Jefferson." He found Jefferson "timid in action; subtle, acute and brilliant in intellect, given to creeping methods. To him, therefore, Marshall, the man of powerful mind, who was as simple and direct as he was absolutely fearless, and who marched straight to his object with his head up and his eyes on his foe, was particularly obnoxious." This statement from the three volumes of hagiography published in 1901 to mark the centennial celebration of Marshall's appointment as chief justice epitomizes the legal fraternity's view of Jefferson and Marshall in a year which was, after all, a centennial for Thomas Jefferson too. George H. Williams, former attorney general of Oregon, went so far then as to assert that while "Jefferson and Madison made some serious mistakes as to matters of government . . . none of any consequence was ever made by Marshall."

With the resurrection of the Democratic party and its great founder, Jefferson, later in the twentieth century, liberal historians have concentrated less upon Jefferson's war on the judiciary and more upon Marshall's war on the executive. Julian Boyd, editor of the magnificent *Papers of Thomas Jefferson* and reader of infinitely more Jeffersoniana than Beveridge, argues that Jefferson disciplined the judiciary for its own good: "Respect for the independence of the judiciary and an understanding of its importance in a government of checks and balances—these enduring convictions rather than personal animus guided Jefferson's hand in this first great crisis over the judiciary. But to the end of his days Marshall saw only the hand and purpose of malignity." Then as now, it would seem, children sometimes rebelled against the "loving" hand which paddled them.

Viewing the Jeffersonian era as an unceasing struggle between Marshall and Jefferson puffs up Marshall and the Supreme Court out of proportion. Marshall helped to make the Supreme Court a great institution, but it did not really become such until after Jefferson's administrations. Marshall and the Marshall Court were an annoyance to President Jefferson, without doubt, but he was too busy with France and

England, with Louisiana and the embargo, to devote extensive attention to the judiciary.

Twice during Jefferson's presidency Judge Marshall assumed major importance—in 1803 when the questions of the Midnight judges and the Midnight justices were settled and in 1807 when Aaron Burr was acquitted of treason charges. At such times, the presence of two such able adversaries at the head of their respective departments assured that there would finally be a searching debate regarding the role of the judiciary and its relationship to the other branches of government. If Marshall was to be a conservative and nationalist balance to Jeffersonian democracy—and he was—he must withstand pressures from the President and the Jeffersonian-dominated Congress—and he did.

❦ 4 ❧

A LAME DUCK
AT MIDNIGHT

———————•┼•———————

A law that has survived for a century is rare indeed, but such distinction does not always mean that it merited that long life. The Judiciary Act of 1789, a tiny segment of which the Marshall Court voided in the *Marbury* v. *Madison* decision, remained the basic foundation of the federal judiciary for more than a century. Senators Oliver Ellsworth and William Paterson, both of whom would later have to learn to live with this law as justices of the United States Supreme Court, have been praised extravagantly for designing a judiciary act which was written for the ages. That the Judiciary Act of 1789 survived without major revision until 1891 was a political and historical accident, however, rather than evidence of its own merits.

THE NEED FOR JUDICIAL REFORM

From the beginning, both judiciary and executive were highly critical of the act and urged its revision. Unfortunately for the Supreme Court, Congress was more content with its handiwork. Only a few months after the law had become effective, President Washington asked the Supreme Court justices for their views of the judicial system, an indication that Washington already had his doubts about it. The justices quickly responded that having members of the Supreme Court serve also in the circuit courts was a serious blunder. Besides being a burden on the judges—who complained privately that Congress treated them as if they were young and vigorous postboys rather than statesmen who had accumulated the years requisite to judiciousness—the Judiciary Act of 1789 presented the anomaly of forcing them to hear on appeals the very cases which they had decided at the lower level. As two of the six justices sat in each circuit court, upon every appeal there was the possibility that one-third of the Court might feel a vested interest in upholding the decision rendered below. This could be prevented only by having that third of the Court stand aside and refuse to participate in an appeals case, thus leaving the decision to four justices or, when there was a division, perhaps only two. Attorney General Edmund Randolph almost immediately submitted to Congress a revised bill which would convert the district judges into circuit judges and leave the Supreme Court justices at the capital, but Congress took no action.

The Supreme Court and the President again tried to persuade Congress in August 1792. All the justices signed a letter to Washington describing burdens "so excessive that we cannot forbear representing them in strong and explicit terms." In a resolution that Washington forwarded to Congress they added that "the task of holding twenty-seven Circuit Courts a year, in the different States, from New Hampshire to Georgia, besides two sessions of the Supreme Court at Philadelphia, in the two most severe seasons of the year [December and August], is a task which, considering the extent of the United States and the small number of Judges, is too burdensome."

In 1793 Congress lightened the burden by requiring that only one justice, rather than two, sit in each circuit court. Still dissatisfied with half a load, the justices requested further relief in 1794, but Congress had done all it intended to do until its hand was forced by politics.

John Jay felt very strongly about the burden of circuit riding—so much so, in fact, that this was the key factor in his decision not to resume his position as chief justice in 1801. He wrote President Adams on January 2 that while the appointment gave him "particular satisfaction" he could not reconcile himself to returning to the old grind. He complained that the Judiciary Act of 1789 was "in some respects more accommodated to certain prejudices and sensibilities, than to the great and obvious principles of sound policy." Because Jay's hopes for its revision had proved in vain, he had resigned, "perfectly convinced that under a system so defective [the judiciary] would not obtain the energy, weight, and dignity which are essential to its affording due support to the national government, nor acquire the public confidence and respect which, as the last resort of the justice of the nation, it should possess." After careful consideration Jay concluded that "the state of my health removes every doubt, it being clearly and decidedly incompetent to the fatigues incident to the office."

MARSHALL AND JUDICIAL REFORM

Ironically, John Marshall played a key role in efforts in 1800 to pass the judicial reform legislation that would have made the chief justiceship more attractive to Jay. Had Congress moved a bit faster, the Jeffersonians might have had to contend with only twenty-eight more years of the Jay Court rather than thirty-four years of the Marshall Court. In December 1799 Adams urged Congress to revise the Judiciary Act; and a solidly Federalist judiciary committee, including John Marshall of Virginia, was promptly set to work in the House.

The committee's proposal was virtually wiped out in March 1800 when the section on restructuring the judicial districts was deleted by a narrow vote. Marshall had argued at length for its retention. If he had been more successful, he might be remembered today as a persuasive minor congressman rather than as "the Great Chief Justice." As early as March 30, 1800, when the judiciary bill was postponed until the next session of Congress, one realistic representative gave a hint of the political handwriting on his wall. He opposed postponement because "the close of the present executive's authority was at hand, and, from his experience, [Adams] was more capable to choose suitable persons to fill the offices than another."

Adams, like Washington, did not give up easily. In his final annual message, which was written by his new secretary of state, John Marshall, he urged upon Congress the "primary importance . . . to the public happiness" of reforming the judiciary. Besides "public happiness," obviously a matter of concern to *all* politicians, an added motivation for Federalists to be prompt in the creation of new judicial offices was the knowledge that all appointments after March 3, 1801, would be made by a Republican, either Thomas Jefferson or Aaron Burr. Vice-President Jefferson wrote Madison on December 26, 1800, of the haste with which the judiciary bill was proceeding through Congress. He dreaded this bill "above all the measures meditated, because appointments in the nature of freehold render it difficult to undo what is done."

A LAME-DUCK JUDICIARY

Federalist politicians were well aware of the need to reform the judiciary before March 1801. Only by gathering all conceivable spoils before the victor assumed office could the vanquished Federalists prevent Jeffersonian "spoilsmanship." Senator William Bingham of Pennsylvania wrote Judge Richard Peters that appointments under the still pending

Judiciary Act *must* be made "under the present administration" because Adams would "give due weight to the Recommendations of the Members of the Senate." To be sure that the Federalist judge did not overlook the obvious, Bingham added that the importance of "filling these Seats with federal characters must be obvious." Senator Dwight Foster of Massachusetts disapproved of efforts "to press this Bill in its present crude State without Amendments," but he could see validity in the argument that "if it now passes Mr. Adams will have the nomination of the Judges to be appointed."

While Adams was still in the process of rewarding deserving Federalists for their promptness in reforming the judiciary, Gouverneur Morris wrote a Republican friend, Robert R. Livingston, to ask if the Federalists should be "blamed for casting many anchors to hold their ship through the storm" when it was obvious that the party was heading into "a heavy gale of adverse wind." Although some improper appointments might occur, this understanding Federalist shrugged, "in what country on earth are all appointments good?" Morris cynically admitted that Federalist leaders probably would "use this opportunity to provide for friends and adherents" and that "if they were my enemies I should condemn them for it."

The sentiments of the job seekers were nicely, if erratically, summed up in a letter which Israel Hatch of Philadelphia addressed to Adams only a week before his administration ended. Requesting almost any office Adams might be willing to offer, Hatch apologized "For not making my Aplication till the Eleventh our" but "If Nothing Should be Don for me by you, I fear your Successor may not comply with my wishes."

The "Act to provide for the more convenient organization of the Courts of the United States" passed the House on January 20 without the backing of a single Republican. The Senate approved it on February 7, and it was signed into law by John Adams on February 13—a Friday. Most important, the new act relieved the Supreme Court justices of their circuit duties and provided new judges specifically for the circuit courts. In addition, the Supreme Court was reduced to five members. Of course a Federalist justice would not be removed —that would be unconstitutional!—but when the first one of the six died or resigned, his place would disappear. Thus some future President—Thomas Jefferson, of course—would be deprived of a Supreme Court appointment. This provision of the Judiciary Act may have been indirectly responsible for the appointment of John Marshall as chief justice. On January 19, 1801, the day that he decided upon Marshall as his nominee, Adams was warned that further delay might deprive him, rather than Jefferson, of the appointment of a sixth justice. "As the bill proposes a reduction of the Judges to five—and as there are already five Judges in commission," Navy Secretary Benjamin Stoddert cautioned him that day, "it is suggested that there might be more difficulty in appointing a chief justice without taking him from the present Judges, after the passage of this bill even by one Branch of the Legislature[,] than before." The next day the House passed the Judiciary Act, and the Senate received Marshall's nomination as chief justice.

The Judiciary Act of 1801 was a commendable piece of legislation though abominably timed. There is general agreement with Justice Harold Burton's conclusion, in an article on the *Marbury* case, that the act "seems well considered." The day before its approval by the Senate, John Marshall praised it for "the separation of the Judges of the supreme from those of the circuit courts, and the establishment of the latter on a system capable of an extension commensurate with the necessities of the nation."

Nevertheless, the stench of dirty politics clung permanently to the Act because of its passage in the last days of the Adams administration. The sheer common sense of having circuit judges preside over circuit courts is obvious, but is it decent to appoint them only days before a repudiated administration leaves office? Not surprisingly, the *Philadelphia Aurora* described the act as "one of the most expensive and extravagant, the most insidious and unnecessary schemes that has been conceived by the Federal party . . . under the name of the Judiciary Bill, but which might with greater propriety be called a bill for providing sinecure places and pensions for thorough-going Federal partisans." Having an odd number of Supreme Court justices to lessen the chance of tie votes is equally desirable, but because of the timing this provision could too easily be and was, of course, regarded as merely a scheme to keep a Republican off the Court. Judicial reform was given such a bad name that for a century Congress could at best only tinker with the judiciary. Finally in 1891 and 1895 Congress made extensive changes which, significantly, reintroduced many features of the repudiated Act of 1801.

Briefly after passage of the Judiciary Act there would be three judges for each of the five major circuits, while one circuit judge would sit in the frontier circuit with the district judges from Kentucky and Tennessee. So long as he did not tarry, Adams would be able to appoint sixteen circuit judges, plus a number of marshals and district attorneys. In addition "An Act concerning the District of Columbia" passed even closer to Midnight, providing for three judges of the circuit court of the District of Columbia and an unlimited number of justices of the peace and other officials. In his last month in office—February being a short month—Adams placed 217 nominations before the Senate. He named 106 (a handful of them recognizable as Republicans) for military and naval positions, 18 for diplomatic and commercial assignments, and 93 for judicial and legal offices. Fifty-three of those in the latter category were appointed to offices in the District of Columbia, including, of course, William Marbury.

The President had hardly begun his task of protecting the country from Jeffersonian officials when he grumbled to his wife that "the Burden upon me in nominating Judges and

Consuls and other officers . . . is and will be very heavy. My time will be taken up." Indeed it was, for he systematically filled the civil offices at his command with Federalists. And of course nearly all federal offices were already occupied by Federalists before he started. One New Yorker, proposing a friend's appointment as a judge, made the correct assumption that Adams would select "Men of legal Abilities, Friends to Govt. & good Order & of unstained moral Character, & Enemies to the fatal Philosophy of the Day." Adams replied that "The character of an enemy to 'the fatal philosophy of the day' has great weight with me, although it appears to have none with our nation."

Besides filling vacancies with right-thinking Federalists, Adams also urged Federalists who had been thinking of resigning to think fast. He did not agree with the view of Lucius H. Stockton, retiring United States attorney for New Jersey and one whom Adams wished to appoint as circuit judge, that in such times "the post of honour . . . is the private station"; but Adams wanted anyone who did feel that way to hurry to the private station before March 4.

Adams' list of judges was highly selective, both in abilities and politics. Any President could take pride in a judiciary containing talents such as those of Egbert Benson, Oliver Wolcott, Jared Ingersoll, Charles Lee, Philip Barton Key, Jeremiah Smith, Theophilus Parsons, and William Tilghman, not all of whom, it should be added, accepted their appointments. But he might also blush at the political one-sidedness of this list. The circuit judges were not outrageous Federalists, for on the whole Adams avoided extremists, but still it is obvious that their political principles and services were the prime requisite of office. Perhaps most reflective of Adams' callousness was the appointment of two former Loyalists to the bench. In fact Philip Barton Key, whose son gained fame as a patriot for writing "The Star Spangled Banner," had led Loyalist troops in the struggle *against* American independence.

MARSHALL AT THE WITCHING HOUR

Second only to Adams himself as a participant in the Midnight Appointments was Chief Justice-Secretary of State John Marshall. It was Secretary Marshall, of course, who applied the Great Seal of the United States to the commissions of office and who, in *most* cases, saw to their delivery; his carelessness in the handling of the justice of the peace commissions for the District of Columbia laid the groundwork for William Marbury's quarrel with the United States government. Besides this ministerial function, Marshall was the major intermediary between the President and Federalists who were recommending nominees. The Adams Papers contain numerous letters addressed to Marshall and obviously forwarded to the President. A large proportion of those who took this avenue to the President was rewarded with offices.

Representative James A. Bayard inadvertently gives an intriguing glimpse into John Marshall's last weeks in the executive department. Bayard remarked late in January, regarding the French treaty, that "The Secretary of State knows as little of the intentions of the President as any other person connected with the Government." Yet, when Bayard was considering whether or not he should accept nomination as minister to France, he consulted at length with Marshall. Both treaties and appointments were proper concerns of the secretary of state, but for the moment the latter were more pressing. Marshall wisely advised Bayard to determine Jefferson's views before accepting an overseas assignment which might last only a matter of days. As might be expected it was a Republican, Robert R. Livingston, who became the new minister to France.

The nefarious nature of Marshall's role at the witching hour between the Adams and Jefferson administrations is fantasied in a piece of household gossip disseminated by Jefferson's great-granddaughter. It depicts Marshall still struggling through a pile of commissions at midnight when Levi Lincoln, who would soon be attorney general and acting secretary of state, stormed in to order Marshall to stop immediately. When they quibbled about the time, the attorney general delivered his first legal opinion—to the chief justice, of all people—by ruling that the President's timepiece, which he held in his hand, was the final authority. The humiliated Marshall then supposedly slunk from the office, leaving a pile of commissions on his desk, including the ill-fated one for William Marbury.

If this melodramatic exchange actually occurred, and a number of Jeffersonian historians have passed it on as though it were historical fact, one must conclude either that President Jefferson did not know the whereabouts of his authoritative watch or that he too had lost track of the time. Later in the month when Jefferson complained about Adams pushing through appointments "with whip and spur" he used identical language in two letters to describe the events of that night. In each he grumbled that Adams was making appointments until "9 o'clock of the night, at 12 o'clock of which he was to go out of office." Had he known of his great-granddaughter's tale, is it conceivable that Jefferson would have omitted the dramatic events of midnight? And without doubt the compendium of political gossip which he called his "Anas" would have included any outrage committed by his old enemy Marshall at the stroke of midnight. Finally, it seems most unlikely that Jefferson would have reappointed the midnight skulker as acting secretary of state, even for a single day. Moreover, if Marshall had somehow regained access to an office from which he had been so dramatically expelled, surely he would have remembered the commissions and taken them with him this time.

James T. Callender found a more legitimate indictment of Marshall when he wrote in the *Richmond Examiner* that "Mr. John Marshall has taken particular care of *his* family." James M. Marshall of Alexandria, brother of and co-speculator with John Marshall, was named a judge for the District of Columbia. Two brothers-in-law of the Judges Marshall, George Keith Taylor of Norfolk, Virginia, and William McClung of Kentucky, became circuit judges. (McClung's principal supporter of record was Senator Humphrey Marshall of Kentucky, a cousin of John Marshall.) Joseph Hamilton Daveiss, who became United States attorney for Kentucky would soon wed still another sister of John Marshall. Either the Marshall girls married *awfully* well or they, themselves, made a splendid catch for office seekers at the turn of the century.

Matthew Lyon, the famous "spitting Lyon" of Vermont, commented on the Marshall clan in an eighteen-page screed, saved for John Adams' first day out of office. He accused Adams of taking "council from the infernal regions" in making nominations. "The greater the villany to be exculpated from, the greater the fee," he charged. According to Lyon, John Marshall therefore received the highest executive office in Adams' hands, that of secretary of state. When this office was made precarious by Jefferson's election

> . . . the Judiciary was the only permanent fund to be applied to, and so long as there was a brother or a sister to make a claim, they, (it seems) have been orderd to draw upon it; Until all were satisfyd—the same fund has served you an excellent purpose for legacies to your poor and distant relatives, as well for rewarding the tories who have been the firmest friends to your administration.*

Depite Lyon's assault—or perhaps because of it—when President Adams left Washington to become "Plain John of Stony Field," he could feel he had plucked some victory from the ashes of electoral defeat by imposing a Federalist judiciary upon the victors. It remained to be seen whether Jefferson would acquiesce in this Midnight counterattack or find ways to push the Federalist judges back into the ashes.

---

* Lyon to Adams, March 4, 1801, Massachusetts Historical Society: Adams Papers.

❦ 5 ❧

JEFFERSONIANS THE
MORNING AFTER

Representative John Randolph described the judiciary left
behind by John Adams as a "hospital of decayed politicians."
Like many another Republican statesman, Randolph would
burn down the "hospital" if necessary to clear out the
"patients." Only a week after the enactment of the Judiciary
Act of 1801, the *National Intelligencer,* the unofficial Jeffersonian journal at Washington, reported "the intention of some
members [of Congress] to effect a repeal of the late judiciary
law." This, despite the fact that the *Intelligencer's* objections to
the judicial appointments were largely procedural.

THE MOVE FOR REPEAL

The likelihood of repeal was evident to Federalists as well.
Two lawyers whom Adams wished to appoint as circuit judges
recognized the danger. Theophilus Parsons of Massachusetts
asked "how long the present system is to last, if it be established
this session"; Lucius H. Stockton of New Jersey added, "It is

true that a Judge cannot be removed from office by a new President but the law under which he is appointed may be repealed by a predominant party." Stockton's comment proved prophetic.

Although Republican newspapers frequently speculated on the badly kept secret that the Judiciary Act would be repealed, President Jefferson said little until December 1801, when a new Congress willing to do his bidding was seated. The month after his inauguration he had written an ally in the Virginia senate that judicial appointments would stand "till the law shall be repealed, which we trust will be at the next Congress." Until then he must content himself with removing only such Midnight appointees as were within his executive power. He wrote Henry Knox, a staunch Massachusetts Federalist and Washington's secretary of war when Jefferson headed the State Department, that while he could not then touch "the life appointments which are irremovable," the other recent appointees were mere nullities who would not even be considered as "candidates for *their* office, much less as possessing it by any title meriting respect." He would not even "pay the respect of notifying them" that they were no longer in office. William Cranch, a circuit judge in the District of Columbia by virtue of Midnight legislation and the beneficence of his father-in-law, John Adams, learned that United States district attorneys who differed with Jefferson's interpretation of the Constitution would be dismissed. Cranch claimed that these "immediate representatives of the President in courts of Justice" must "believe every thing to be unconstitutional which the President thinks to be so." As the judiciary was inundated with Federalism, Jefferson insisted that the prosecuting attorneys be at least a small island of Republicanism. In April 1801 he wrote that "the only shield for Republican citizens against the federalism of the courts is to have the Attornies & Marshals republicans." The justices of the peace for the District of Columbia did not seem to fit into Jefferson's classification of officials serving at the President's pleasure, but Marshall's carelessness in leaving behind their commissions gave Jefferson the opportunity to disregard their appointments, thus creating the *Marbury* case.

President Jefferson finally dropped his other shoe on the Midnight judges on December 8, 1801, in his first annual message to Congress. Jefferson's language was veiled, though his message was transparent to the enthusiastic Republicans who had finally gained control of Congress: "The judiciary system of the United States, and especially that portion of it recently erected, will of course present itself to the contemplation of Congress." To aid Congress in its deliberations Jefferson included a list of cases decided and pending in federal courts. This was, of course, designed to prove that the new courts were a reckless extravagance. A week later, in a private letter, Jefferson gave a better idea of his reasons for wanting the Judiciary Act repealed. The Federalist party had "retired into the Judiciary as a strong hold," he complained.

> There the remains of federalism are to be preserved & fed from the treasury, and from that battery all the works of republicanism are to be beaten down & erased. by a fraudulent use of the constitution which has made judges irremoveable, they have multiplied useless judges merely to strengthen their phalanx.*

From January to March 1802 Congress engaged in a searching debate which has been unequaled in the history of its relations with the federal judiciary. Not until 1937, when Franklin D. Roosevelt sought to "pack" (or "reform") the Supreme Court, did Congress again examine the judicial function so comprehensively. The Jeffersonian Republicans had the votes to control Congress, just as the Federalists had in 1801, but the minority in 1802 was not as acquiescent as the Republicans had been when the Judiciary Act of 1801 was passed.

Two main questions had to be answered before repealing the Act: Could Congress abolish previously established courts

---

* Jefferson to John Dickinson, December 19, 1801, The Historical Society of Pennsylvania.

and judicial positions; and, if it could, what would become of the judges whose term was established by the Constitution as "during good Behaviour"? Debate centered on the latter question, because even the Federalists were weak on the former. They had, after all, done away with some courts created in 1789 when they rearranged the judiciary, even if they had thoughtfully provided any judge who lost his bench with a better one. The Virginia Republican philosopher John Taylor of Caroline incredulously asked of the "good Behaviour" requirement: "Could it mean that he should hold office after it had been abolished? Could it mean that his tenure should be limited by behaving well in an office which did not exist?" For Federalists the answer was "yes"; for the Republican majority in Congress it was "no."

Even so, Governor James Monroe of Virginia seems to have felt that the Republican congressmen had not gone far enough. He criticized their admission that "the Legislature has not a right to repeal the law organizing the Supreme Court, for the express purpose of dismissing the Judges, when they cease to possess the publick confidence." While the executive might seduce the judges with other appointments, the Legislature "or in other words, the people, have no checks whatever on them, no means of counteracting that seduction but impeachment, to which it may be difficult to resort for mere political depravity." Even if Supreme Court justices could be removed without the nuisance of impeachment, and Monroe's mind was not then "made up on this point," he saw no need for removals in 1802. Monroe was concerned, however, that Congress was denying itself a power which might at some later period be necessary.

THE CONTROVERSY OVER JUDICIAL REVIEW

The debates in Congress were in many respects a prelude to the *Marbury* v. *Madison* case. Congress was well aware

of issues which would be coming before the Supreme Court;
Federalist legislators were happy to advise what the judges
should do, while Republicans in Congress warned what
would happen to the judges if they followed the Federalists'
advice. Federalists were confident that the judiciary must find
the repeal law unconstitutional because it removed from office
judges whose behavior had been "good." The tradition is that
the black-robed magician, John Marshall, virtually pulled
judicial review out of a hat, that it was something novel when
he announced it in 1803. On the contrary, the voiding of
legislation for constitutional reasons was discussed extensively
and heatedly in Congress a year before the *Marbury* decision.
Representative James A. Bayard of Delaware, for instance,
warned that if the Constitution is to survive there must be "a
power to which the acknowledged right is attached of pro-
nouncing the invalidity of the acts of the Legislature which
contravene the instrument." After considering federal and
state legislatures and state courts, Bayard concluded that the
only appropriate body for this essential charge was the federal
judiciary. Federalist Representative Archibald Henderson of
North Carolina was appalled by "the monstrous and unheard
of" contention of Republicans that the Supreme Court could
not void unconstitutional legislation. If they succeeded in
killing judicial review, the United States government would
be a "tyranny" and its people "slaves." It was fitting that
Gouverneur Morris of New York led the advocates of judicial
review in the Senate, for when he was asked in 1787 if the
Federal Convention had come forth with "a good Constitution," he replied: "That depends on how it is construed." He
was confident in 1802 that the Supreme Court would not
"neglect doing the great mischief of saving this Constitution"
by preventing Congress from "passing an unconstitutional
law." Like Marshall in *Marbury* v. *Madison,* Morris believed
that judicial authority to void such legislation was "derived
from authority higher than this Constitution. They derive it

from the constitution of man, from the nature of things, from the necessary progress of human affairs." Clearly natural rights was not a private Jeffersonian preserve. Both Morris and Bayard warned that if Congress became the final interpreter of the Constitution it would be sovereign, rather than the American people.

Senator James Ross of Pennsylvania, who had participated in this debate, restated the Federalist argument succinctly when the issue came briefly before Congress again in 1803, shortly before the *Marbury* trial:

> Either the law or the constitution is a nullity. If the new doctrines be true the law must prevail. If so, why provide any prohibitions or exceptions in a Constitution, and why ask any solemn pledge to support it? The Court, when pressed for its judgment, must declare which shall prevail, and if they do their duty they will certainly say, that a law at variance with the Constitution is utterly void; it is made without authority and cannot be executed. By doing so the courts do not control or prostrate the just authority of Congress. It is the will of the people expressed in the Constitution which controls them.*

Just three weeks later John Marshall would say the same thing, at infinitely greater length, in the *Marbury* decision.

The same philosophy was prevalent among Federalists outside of Congress. Alexander Hamilton, for instance, urged that repeal of the Judiciary Act be tested before the Supreme Court "as soon as possible." The *Washington Federalist,* a newspaper with which Marshall had close ties, urged that the circuit judges "continue to hold their courts as if the bill had not passed. 'Tis their solemn duty to do it; their country, all that is dear and valuable, call upon them to do it. By the judges this bill will be declared null and void." If the circuit judges had been so daring, the Marshall Court would have found it difficult to avoid a head-on collision with the Jefferson administration and Congress.

---

* *Annals of Congress,* 7th Cong., 2d sess., 70–71 (February 3, 1803).

In the judicial controversy, as in so many other party struggles of the Jefferson administration, Virginia and Kentucky congressmen led the attack. Even though Senator John Breckenridge had only recently introduced and advocated Jefferson's Kentucky Resolutions in his state legislature, he insisted now that the "pretended power of the Courts to annul the laws of Congress cannot possibly exist" because *Congress* had "the exclusive right to interpret the Constitution, in what regards the law-making power, and the judges are bound to execute the laws they make." In 1798, when the Federalists had controlled Congress, Breckenridge and the Kentucky Resolutions contended that the states, not Congress, should interpret the Constitution. He thought it "extraordinary" that if a power of judicial review was intended it was not specified in the Constitution.

Although today we recognize judicial review as an essential element of the *Marbury* decision, no one in Congress, Federalist or Republican, could have foreseen its relationship to this case. Probably Marshall himself did not know in 1802 that William Marbury would be the lever which he would use to squeeze judicial review into American constitutional history.

William Marbury and the uncommissioned justices were thrust directly into the controversy over the repeal of the Judiciary Act of 1801 almost from the beginning. In December 1801, as a preliminary to the case, Chief Justice Marshall directed Secretary of State Madison to show cause at the next session of the Supreme Court why a writ of mandamus should not be issued requiring delivery of the commissions. Madison ignored the directive, but Republican partisans in Congress were outraged at this breach of the separation of powers. A Republican correspondent wrote the *Salem Register* that the "late mandamus business in the supreme court was calculated expressly with a view to deter from any attempt to repeal" the Judiciary Act. If this were true, and it seems most unlikely because Marshall was merely following normal procedure, it was very poor strategy.

Senator Stevens Thomson Mason of Virginia wrote Governor Monroe that the Supreme Court had attempted to "assail the Presdt (through the sides of Mr Madison) ." Mason predicted that Republican indignation in Congress would "secure the repeal of the judiciary law of the last Session, about the propriety of which some of our Republican friends were hesitating." Senator Breckenridge made Mason a good prophet. Complaining to Monroe on December 24 about the judges' "daring attack," he added that he wanted "the subject of the Courts to be brought forward in the Senate next week." On January 6, 1802, Breckenridge himself moved the repeal act. It was fitting that a Kentuckian take the lead, for many from this state feared that the new courts would impose unwelcome order on the chaos of Kentucky land titles.

Virginia congressmen frequently roasted the Supreme Court for its order to Madison. William Branch Giles reminded the House of Representatives that the Court had dared to send a "mandatory process into the Executive cabinet, to examine its concerns." "Does this," he demanded, "seem unambitious?" Representative John Randolph mocked the pretensions of these "harmless unaspiring men," which extended *only* to "a complete exemption from Legislative control; to the exercise of an inquisitorial authority over the Cabinet of the Executive, and the veto of the Roman Tribunate upon all your laws." Senator Stevens Thomson Mason warned that if the Supreme Court were permitted to "hold the Constitution in one hand, and the law in the other, and say to the departments of Government, so far shall you go and no farther," the judges would have converted judicial independence into "something like supremacy."

REPEAL

The Senate repealed the Judiciary Act of 1801 on February 3, 1802, by a sixteen-to-fifteen party vote. Every Federal-

ist opposed the measure, and every Republican but one
supported it. Exactly a month later the House of Representatives concurred, again with a single Republican
holdout.

During the debates in the House, Representative James A.
Bayard warned the Republicans that repeal of the Judiciary
Act might bring armed resistance. "There are many, very
many, who believe, if you strike this blow, you inflict a mortal
wound on the Constitution. There are many now willing to
spill blood to defend that Constitution." Fortunately, the
Federalists only decried the repeal rather than waging war to
prevent it. (As far afield as Bayard's warning, but in the opposite direction, was the *National Intelligencer*'s smug assumption that "not one man in a thousand will condemn the
repealing act.") Federalist Gouverneur Morris wrote most of
his correspondents that the repeal act had destroyed the
Constitution. "We have here as yet done nothing of importance," he wrote Republican Robert R. Livingston, "except
destroying the Constitution by repealing the judiciary law of
last session." The pro-Marshall *Washington Federalist,* in "A
LONG FAREWELL, TO ALL OUR GREATNESS," expected
the abolition of the Supreme Court soon to follow—"Such
is democracy." The Hamiltonian *Gazette of the United
States* reported that despair in Washington was such that
property could no longer be sold. The "sober-minded men
of Virginia" were trying unsuccessfully to sell their land
and move to New England as the sole remaining haven
against Jacobinism.

Despite admonitions to break the law (the repeal law) by
serving as if their courts still existed, the circuits judges dared
only to submit an appeal for relief to the Congress which had
just unseated them. As might have been expected, the Republican Congress found this appeal resistible. A proposal to
submit the petition "to judicial decision" was voted down 57
to 35 in the House.

JUDICIAL RESPONSE TO REPEAL

If the 1801-style judiciary was to be resurrected, it must be
done by the Supreme Court, and the Republicans quickly took
precautions to prevent this. In April 1802, after shockingly
scanty debate, Congress amended the now-restored Judiciary
Act of 1789. It relieved the Supreme Court justices of some of
their burdens and, incidentally, put the Court out of business
for thirteen months. The circuits were reorganized to make
circuit riding less rigorous for the justices, and henceforth the
Supreme Court itself would have only one session annually,
in February. The Judiciary Act of 1801 had provided June and
December sessions, in place of the February and August
terms established in 1789. Of course anyone would be relieved to avoid going to Washington, D.C., in the summers.
The aged Cushing was especially pleased, but Marshall, too,
considered the new judicial arrangements "less burdensome
than heretofore, or than I expected." As good Federalists, however, they were dismayed that Congress had, in effect, gagged
the Court for thirteen months. Marshall expressed his regret
that "the next June term will be put down" in a letter to one
of the unfrocked circuit judges, Oliver Wolcott. February had
already passed; there would be no June, August, or December
session, so the Supreme Court would remain silent from
December 1801 to February 1803. Besides delaying the *Marbury*
v. *Madison* case for eight months, Congress prevented any
timely response to the repeal of the Judiciary Act of 1801. If
the Court persisted in ruling upon the repeal, by February
1803 it would be serving up warmed-over stew.

Republican precautions to prevent the Supreme Court from
speaking out against the repeal of the Judiciary Act at least
implied that the Supreme Court *might,* if it *could,* exercise
judicial review. Representative James A. Bayard chided the
Republicans for viewing the justices as "objects of terror." He
warned that a thirteen-month hiatus for the Supreme Court

might be followed by its "virtual abolition." "If the functions of the court can be extended by law for fourteen [sic] months, what time will arrest us before we arrive at ten or twenty years?" Joseph H. Nicholson of Maryland, who led the debate for the Republicans, professed "unconcern whether they pronounce the repealing law unconstitutional or not," but he added, significantly, that the Republicans had as much "right to suppose gentlemen on the other side are as anxious for a session in June, that this power may be exercised, as they have to suppose we wish to avoid it, to prevent the exercise." As influential a Republican as James Monroe feared that postponement of the Supreme Court session might be regarded as cowardly evasion by Congress. It might give "new colour" to the judges' "pretensions, new spirits to their party, and a better prospect of success." He would rather see the Republicans take "a bold attitude and apparently invite" a collision with the Supreme Court than to avoid it by stealth.

Although Chief Justice Marshall appears to have been a major force in cooling the ardor of the "repealed" judges, he attempted to persuade his brethren of the Supreme Court to risk a show of force against the Jeffersonians by refusing to resume their circuit duties. After an effusive profession to Justice Paterson of his respect for those (including Paterson) "who passed the original law concerning the courts of the United States and those who first acted under it," Marshall declared that Congress had acted unconstitutionally in again imposing circuit duties on the Supreme Court and that the Court had shirked its responsibilities by accepting this unconstitutional assignment. Although the consequences of refusing to sit in circuit court "may be very serious," Marshall would disregard them if he had the support of the associate justices: "Duty first, now is the time to act if ever."

The other justices, with the possible but unlikely exception of Albert Moore whose response is not known, agreed that the Constitution requires distinct appointments and commissions for judges of the Supreme Court and the circuit courts. Their interpretation was that since the Constitution established a *Supreme* Court, by implication it likewise provided for inferior courts and for judges to occupy those benches. Only Samuel Chase, however, was willing to mount the barricades with Marshall to defend this principle. Chase was far more belligerent then, as always, than Marshall. He wanted the Supreme Court to meet in August to prepare a resolution for the President. Next, the Midnight judges were to bring forward a suit to regain either their offices or salaries. Finally, the justices should refuse to take the circuit; Chase intended to refuse unless persuaded otherwise by his brethren.

In his letter to Paterson, Marshall hit upon the problem which the other associates would regard as insurmountable in making a constitutional issue of their circuit duties. The fact that the Supreme Court justices had for a decade sat in the circuit courts would vastly weaken their argument that to serve there again would be unconstitutional. Regarding a remonstrance, Cushing reminded Chase that the President need only reply that he could not control Congress—and "you & I know" that the Supreme Court "cannot control the Majority." The Marshall Court did little to please Louis Boudin in his two-volume attack on judicial review, but Boudin does luxuriate in the justices' refusal in 1802 to risk possible impeachment or removal by voiding a law which they privately agreed was unconstitutional. This timidity put the Supreme Court justices exactly where Boudin wanted them, for "the entire argument" in favor of permitting courts to rule laws unconstitutional is based on the belief that judges are "a superior breed of men" who would never fear to "risk the consequences" of their actions. And as for Marshall, there was nothing to prevent him from setting a brave example by refusing to sit in the circuit courts and thus "risk the consequences" all by himself.

Although the Supreme Court decided unofficially, and thus privately, in the spring of 1802 that it would not interfere in the repeal of the Judiciary Act, Jeffersonians remained in suspense for a year longer. Ironically, the case which finally necessitated an official pronouncement was a Virigina land case appealed from the Fifth Circuit, presided over by the unwilling John Marshall. To the protest that the Stuart v. Laird, 1 Cranch 299 (1803), case could not be transferred to the new-old circuit court and that the presence in this court of a Supreme Court justice was unconstitutional, Judge Marshall had merely replied that the plea was insufficient and forwarded it to the Supreme Court on a writ of error. Thus, simultaneously with the *Marbury* v. *Madison* case, the Supreme Court received its supposedly long-awaited opportunity to speak out on the constitutionality of the judiciary repeal act.

Representing the plaintiffs was Charles Lee of Virginia, a close personal friend of Marshall, attorney general in the Adams administration, and a Federalist who had wisely declined appointment as a Midnight judge to return to private practice. He asserted that the repeal was unconstitutional because it deprived "the courts of all their power and jurisdiction, and . . . displace[d] judges who have been guilty of no misbehavior in their offices." The later Judiciary Act, which returned circuit responsibilities to the Supreme Court, was also unconstitutional because "no act of congress can extend the original jurisdiction of the Supreme Court beyond the bounds limited by the constitution." Being "totally unconstitutional, they are void." He quoted high authority—James Madison and John Marshall in the Virginia ratifying convention of 1788— to prove the inviolability of the judiciary. Finally, in hopes of offsetting the argument of precedent, the principal threat to his case, Lee declared that "if it be said that the practice from the year 1789 to 1801 is against us, we answer that the practice was wrong, that it crept in unawares, without consideration and without opposition."

William Paterson answered for the Supreme Court on March 2, only six days after Marshall delivered the *Marbury* decision. Marshall did not participate in *Stuart* v. *Laird* be-

cause he had "tried the cause in the court below." Regarding
the rearrangement of the circuits, Paterson said that "Congress
have constitutional authority to establish from time to time
such inferior tribunals as they may think proper"; regarding
the sitting of a Supreme Court justice in a circuit court, he
ruled that "practice and acquiescence under it for a period of
several years, commencing with the organization of the judicial
system, affords an irresistible answer, and indeed fixed the
construction. . . . Of course, the question is at rest," he concluded, "and ought not now to be disturbed."

At last the Jeffersonians could be certain that the judiciary
would not wage open warfare against them. The guerrilla
tactics of *Marbury* v. *Madison* would not escalate into all-out
war. Jeffersonian relief is evident in the major Republican
newspapers' praise to Marshall for proving that he would not
"surrender the chastity of the Court to the lust of envy." This
remark was in the most searching Republican criticism of
Marbury v. *Madison*, a series of letters by "Littleton" in the
Virginia Argus, which was reprinted in most Republican journals, including the powerful *National Intelligencer* and *Philadelphia Aurora*. In his fourth letter, Littleton contrasted the
"grotesque" *Marbury* v. *Madison* with the praiseworthy *Stuart*
v. *Laird,* praising Marshall for calming "the tumult of faction"
in the latter case and standing, as he "must continue to stand,
a star of the first magnitude." Unfortunately for Marshall, this
rare and rhapsodical Republican praise was for a decision in
which he did not participate. The outcome of *Stuart* v. *Laird*
was as surprising as that of *Marbury* v. *Madison*. The relief
Republicans gained from the Midnight judge decision helped
to offset some of the resentments caused by the Midnight
justice decision.

✦ 6 ✦

JUSTICES AND INJUSTICES

———————————•◆•———————————

The Act Concerning the District of Columbia is of little importance compared with the Judiciary Act of 1801. If it had not led directly to the important constitutional case of *Marbury* v. *Madison,* it would be a footnote in the most local of local history. Writing on February 25, 1801, to his Aunt Abigail Adams, William S. Shaw placed the bill in what *seemed* to be its proper perspective: "No laws of national importance have been enacted since you left us. A bill has passed the house respecting this district, which I understand to be a mere system of judicature only." Billy Shaw, who was then secretary to his Uncle John Adams, was as impressed by the bill's significance as the legislators who had just hustled it through Congress with scarcely any debate. The Senate passed the measure on February 5, and the House on February 24, 1801. Adams signed it three days later, leaving him only four days to fill the offices it created in the District of Columbia.

Because the District of Columbia bill was so unmemorable, historians have often confused Marbury and company with the Midnight judges of the Judiciary Act of 1801. Only a few months prior to the publication of his important biography of John Marshall, for instance, Albert J. Beveridge still believed that the *Marbury* case grew out of the Judiciary Act of 1801. He wrote in 1919 to the historian J. Franklin Jameson, who fortunately corrected him, that if Marshall had not exercised judicial review in the *Marbury* case he would have been "compelled to either recognize the validity of the Republican repeal ... or else he would have been compelled to hold the Repeal unconstitutional." An earlier historian of note, John Bach McMaster, confused the case by protraying the four plaintiffs—William Marbury, Dennis Ramsay, Robert Townshend Hooe, and William Harper—as the sole Adams appointees as justices of the peace for the District of Columbia. A more common error, stemming from reference only to Marbury in Marshall's decision, is to treat the case as if Marbury were the sole protagonist.

FEDERALIST JUSTICES OF THE PEACE

It could have been taken for granted that the departing John Adams would find more than four Federalists to honor. He was authorized by the District of Columbia Act to appoint "such number of discreet persons to be justices of the peace, as the President of the United States shall from time to time think expedient, to continue in the office five years." He found it expedient—politically, if not otherwise—to appoint forty-two justices of the peace, twenty-three for Washington County on the Maryland side of the Potomac River and nineteen for Alexandria County on the Virginia side. There were only 8,144 persons (nearly one-fourth slaves) in Washington County and 7,121 (more than one-sixth slaves) in Alexandria County, so President Adams was thoughtfully supplying these counties with a justice of the peace for every 363½ persons, irrespective of age, sex, color, or condition of servitude.

Accompanying the justice of the peace nominations sent to the Senate and rapidly confirmed on March 2 were nominations of three circuit judges for the district and a number of lesser officials. The two associate judges had impeccable credentials, William Cranch being the son-in-law of John Adams and James M. Mashall the brother of John Marshall. There was little antagonism to these appointments, however, and in 1805 Cranch was advanced to chief judge by Jefferson. As unofficial reporter for the United States Supreme Court, Cranch is our major source of information on *Marbury* v. *Madison* and contemporary cases. Adams did less well when he looked outside the family, because his selection for chief judge, Thomas Johnson, declined the appointment and left a rare vacancy for Jefferson to fill in March 1801. John Marshall was "excessively mortified" by Johnson's refusal: "There was a negligence in that business arising from a confidence that Mr. Johnston [sic] woud accept, which I lament excessively."

It is not surprising that Adams, in his spur-of-the-moment appointments to an office of limited importance in a district of limited population, should have located few men of reputation to serve as justices of the peace. There are some familiar names, such as Benjamin Stoddert, Daniel Carroll (who was related by marriage to John Marshall), William Thornton, William Fitzhugh, and Tristram Dalton, but most of those named are as unknown as William Marbury would have been had Thomas Jefferson kept him out of constitutional history by permitting him to serve his justiceship in peace. Few bothered to apply for the office, though one Marylander later complained to Adams that he had been "told by a Gentleman of Veracity, who saw it, that I was in the nomination in the List made out by you, but in the Publication in the news papers after you left this, I was Left out all to gether."

Maryland and Virginia congressmen made their wishes known to the executive, however. The most demanding, and the most successful, was Representative Leven Powell of northern Virginia, who sent twelve names to Marshall with the request that "you will be pleased to send in the names of these gentlemen to the President of the United States for his consideration." All twelve were among the nineteen names which Adams submitted to Congress. Perhaps Powell could have done even better if he had dreamed that Adams would appoint so many justices from Alexandria. The President may have been especially sympathetic to Powell because in 1796 he was the only Virginia elector to vote for Adams, and thus against Jefferson. Adams hated to be known as "President by three votes," but it would have been worse to be President by one vote, which he would have been if Powell had not been a Virginia elector. The fact that four of the eight nominees from whom Jefferson later withheld commissions were among those advanced by Powell was probably merely a coincidence. Jefferson probably could not have known whom Powell suggested or even that he made nominations.

THE CARELESSNESS OF
SECRETARY MARSHALL

Secretary of State John Marshall was kept busier than he would have liked to be on the last day of the Adams administration, for it was the responsibility of the secretary of state to place the Great Seal of the United States upon commissions after the President had signed them and then to see to their delivery. Signing and sealing went on schedule, but in the bustle of concluding his executive duties Marshall neglected to deliver the commissions of the justices of the peace. Thus the final blunder of Secretary of State Marshall led directly to the first "triumph" of Chief Justice Marshall.

Marshall served momentarily as secretary of state in the Jefferson administration at Jefferson's special request. Had his memory been better, he might have prevented the *Mar-*

bury case by thinking to pick up the forgotten commissions on March 4. Piling irony on top of irony, Judge Marshall—James Marshall—visited the office of the secretary of state that morning to pick up several of the commissions. Riotous conduct is not entirely a twentieth-century accompaniment to presidential inaugurations; Judge James Marshall anticipated trouble in Alexandria, so he took the initiative in activating some justices of the peace on the chance they might be needed. He signed a receipt for several commissions, twelve of the nineteen Alexandria commissions, he believed. For some reason James Marshall decided he "could not conveniently carry the whole"—more likely he felt physically unable to *deliver* all that he had—so he returned a handful and crossed out those names from his receipt. Among those returned were commissions for Robert Townshend Hooe and William Harper, who would soon unite with William Marbury and Dennis Ramsay to appeal their loss to the United States Supreme Court. Judge William Cranch wrote his father-in-law, John Adams, that Marshall had taken only "2 or 3" commissions, though it is likely that Marshall's testimony would have indicated this if he had taken so few.

The Marshall brothers, then, shared both in the concern and the responsibility for the plight of the commissionless justices of the peace. The chief justice wrote to the judge two weeks after Jefferson's assumption of power to voice his "infinite chagrin" over Jefferson's decision to hold back the commissions. His regret was increased by the fact that "I fear some blame may be imputed to me." He explained further:

> I did not send out the commissions because I apprehended such as were for a fixd time to be completed when signd & seald & such as depended on the will of the President might at any time be revokd. To with hold the commission of the Marshal is equal to displacing him which the President I presume has the power to do; but to with hold the commission of the Justices is an act of which

I entertaind no suspicion. I shoud however have sent out the commissions which had been signd & seald but for the extreme hurry of the time & the absence of Mr. Wagner who had been calld on by the President to act as his private secretary.*

Jacob Wagner, a clerk in the office of the secretary of state, would be an unwilling witness two years later when Marbury's attorney, Charles Lee, had the peculiar task of proving to Chief Justice Marshall that the missing commissions had actually been signed and sealed, but without implicating Secretary of State Marshall. What interesting reading this letter from Justice Marshall to Judge Marshall would have been for the harried Lee!

John Adams concurred in Marshall's view that delivery of a commission was not essential to an officer's appointment. But however confident of the rights of the aspiring justices to their signed and sealed commissions, experienced politicians such as John Marshall and John Adams should have recognized that, after cynically depriving President Jefferson of every conceivable opportunity to make his own appointments, the outgoing administration should have left *no* unfinished business.

JEFFERSON'S JUSTICES OF THE PEACE

Naturally, when Attorney General Levi Lincoln, who was acting secretary of state while James Madison was detained in Virginia by the death of his father, reported to President Jefferson that the justice of the peace commissions were still in the State Department, Jefferson ordered them held up. Marshall should have been surprised by Jefferson's moderation after Midnight, instead of by the withholding of the commissions. Rather than throwing out all forty-two of Adams' appointees, Jefferson issued omnibus commissions, one for Washington County and one for Alexandria County, which

* John Marshall to James M. Marshall, March 18, 1801, Library of Congress: Marshall Papers.

omitted only 40 percent of Adams' Midnight justices. Complaining that forty-two justices were "too numerous," he cut the number to fifteen for each county. Nine of Adams' nominees were omitted and Jefferson added only one name for Washington County. For Alexandria County, which was more familiar territory to Jefferson, he omitted eight Adams appointees and added four new names.

Even though the justices of the peace would be the District of Columbia's principal governing body outside the towns of Alexandria and Georgetown, there was little excitement either when Adams filled the offices or when Jefferson emptied some of them. The Jeffersonian *National Intelligencer,* for instance, listed the Adams nominees on March 9, 1801, without comment. Nine days later it listed Jefferson's nominees, again without comment. On March 23 it justly praised Jefferson's moderation in pruning the Adams list. Finally, on April 3 the *National Intelligencer* printed a lengthy essay which adopted Jefferson's arguments for withholding the commissions. The Federalist *Alexandria Gazette* displayed even less concern. It listed the Adams appointees on March 9 without editorial comment or local allusions, and it did not discuss the issue again until February 1803, when the affair had transcended local government and become a constitutional case.

Nor were the appointees, themselves, quaking in fear lest they be denied a commission. Three of the Adams appointees who were finally included in the Jefferson commissions refused to serve either because the office itself or perhaps the necessity of accepting it from Jefferson was beneath their dignity. The office of justice of the peace was well toward the bottom of the barrel of political plums. Its civil jurisdiction was limited to cases of "the value of twenty dollars, exclusive of costs," and the pay was by fees rather than salary. Charles Lee said as much when he argued the *Marbury* case before the Supreme Court: "The emoluments, or the dignity of the office, are no objects with the applicants." Besides, two years of the five-year terms had already passed by then. As any lawyer who is presenting a cause which "may seem trivial at first view must do," Lee argued that the *Marbury* case was "important in principle." It was Marshall, however, who made the case important, not Lee or Marbury.

Jefferson later described *Marbury* v. *Madison* as "a moot case," because Marbury sued for a valueless office. Yet Jefferson recognized that the office could be important politically even if it was not economically. He was well aware that in neighboring Virginia the office of justice of the peace was the starting point of significant political careers. Charles Sydnor, describing "The Pathway to Power" in Virginia politics in his *Gentlemen Freeholders,* regards "admission to the office of justice of the peace and thus to a seat on the bench of the county court" as "the first upward step in a political career" in Virginia. Jefferson himself had taken this first step, as had George Washington, James Madison, James Monroe, George Wythe, George Mason, and most other prominent figures in early Virginia. Monroe would even serve as a justice *after* leaving the White House. John Marshall was one of those very rare statesmen who by-passed the office.

Years later Jefferson described the county courts as the most dangerous branch of Virginia government. "The vicious constitution of our county courts (to whom the justice, the executive administration, the taxation, the police, the military appointments of the county, and nearly all our daily concerns are confided)" were, he contended, "self-appointed, self-continued, holding their authorities for life, and with an impossibility of breaking in on the perpetual succession of any faction once possessed of the bench. They are in truth, the executive, the judiciary, and the military of their respective counties, and the sum of the counties make the State." Jefferson's moderate handling of the Adams commissions is more remarkable in light of his experience with the political possibilities of this office in Virginia.

Seventeen Federalists were deprived of their commissions as justices of the peace for the District of Columbia, but only four bothered to press their case in the courts. These four—William Marbury, Robert Townshend Hooe, Dennis Ramsay, and William Harper—epitomize the economic and political interests of the Federalist party.

WILLIAM MARBURY

William Marbury came from a well-known Maryland family, but the better known Marburys were from other branches of the family tree. Like most other residents of the Maryland side of the District of Columbia, Marbury was a recent arrival. He was thirty-seven years old in 1799 when he was appointed navy agent to oversee the vessels at the marine hospital reservation at Washington. He moved then from Annapolis to the District of Columbia, where he built a large house on Falls Street. He invested wisely in District of Columbia land and soon became a large landowner. These investments involved Marbury in transportation projects, such as building the Eastern Branch Bridge connecting Washington with Uniontown, property (across the Anacostia River from the navy yard) that he also owned. For a number of years he was a leading figure in the Potomac Company, a venture led by George Washington which was intended to link the Potomac and Ohio rivers. When his case first appeared before the Supreme Court, the *Philadelphia Aurora* contemptuously described Marbury as "one of those concerned with Stoddart, Forrest, & c. who have made so much noise in the contracts for timber, and banking affairs." He was a director of the Bank of Columbia throughout the Jefferson administrations. In February 1814, six months before the British blackened Washington in "Mr. Madison's War," Marbury became the first president of the Farmers and Mechanics National Bank in Georgetown.

Marbury was more fortunate the second time he appeared

before the Marshall Court in 1822. Marshall wrote the opinion in *Marbury* v. *Brooke,* a case involving Marbury's trusteeship of the property of a fugitive forger. Marbury's son-in-law, Richard H. Fitzhugh, forged the notes of several banks, including the Farmers and Mechanics National Bank where he signed Marbury's name. Marbury had intended to cover up for Fitzhugh until he learned it would cost far more than the $5,000 or $6,000 which he had anticipated. Also, the Federalist Bank of the United States apparently intended to prosecute Fitzhugh, regardless of what his father-in-law did. Marbury and his son John, a lawyer, advised Fitzhugh to flee the District of Columbia. As trustee, the elder Marbury supervised the distribution of Fitzhugh's scanty belongings among his many creditors, an arrangement which the Marshall decision upheld. Marbury lived for thirty-two years after his name had been immortalized by John Marshall in *Marbury* v. *Madison* in 1803. He died in March 1835, less than four months before Marshall's own demise.

HOOE, RAMSAY, AND HARPER

The next best known of the four dissatisfied justices of the peace is Robert Townshend Hooe. The Hooe family's widespread commercial interests were so significant that even President Jefferson made purchases from "Messrs. Robert Hooe & co." even if Robert T. Hooe did not merit a commission as justice of the peace. Although he could not get his commission from the Supreme Court, 1803 was a good year for Hooe, judicially speaking. In that same session of the Supreme Court he won the admiralty case of Hooe & Co. v. Groverman, 1 Cranch 214 (1803), and the bond penalty case of United States v. R. T. Hooe and others, 1 Cranch 318 (1803).

Hooe was mayor of Alexandria from 1780 to 1782 and sheriff of Fairfax County in 1790. In December 1789, before the government under the United States Constitution was a year old, Hooe was one of several "boosters" who pressed the advantages of Alexandria-Georgetown as the site of the new national capital. Hooe speculated in western lands and also owned much land in and around the District of Columbia. The will he filed in 1796 listed 102,400 acres in Kentucky and another 4,870 acres in western Virginia. In addition, he owned a number of town lots, mostly in Alexandria. At the time of his short-lived emergence as a justice of the peace he was advertising to sell western land or exchange it for Alexandria, Washington, or Fairfax county lots. Like Marbury, Hooe was involved in the Potomac Company. He realized early the awkwardness of being a slave-owning Quaker and therefore emancipated his slaves. Hooe died in 1809, leaving the bulk of his landed estate to his cousin and partner, Richard Harrison.

Dennis Ramsay seems to have been the moving force for the three aborted Alexandria justices. He filed affidavits in December 1801 for himself and the other two justices. Like so many other Virginia Federalists, Ramsay had fallen under the spell of General Washington during the Revolutionary War. He advanced from the rank of captain to colonel in the Virginia Continental Line. And like so many other Scottish Virginians he early became a merchant. Before the Revolution eighteen-year-old Dennis Ramsay entered the firm of Jennifer & Hooe (!) at Dumfries, Virginia. He was mayor of Alexandria in 1788–1789 (and again in 1792–1794) and delivered the town's farewell address to its favorite son George Washington when he departed to become President of the United States. Ramsay was an honorary pallbearer for Washington ten years later. His leanings toward what would become Federalist economics are shown by his participation in petitions to allow increased power over commerce by the Continental Congress in 1785 and to urge Virginia to incorporate a bank at Alexandria in 1792. Like Marbury, Harper, and Hooe, he was a subscriber to the Potomac Company. Ramsay died in Alexandria in 1810 at the age of fifty-four.

William Harper was the least persistent of the four appellants. He was the only one who neglected to deliver the court order of December 21, 1801, directing Madison to show cause why he should not be forced to deliver the commissions. Harper also sat out the second round, when Marbury, Ramsay, and Hooe petitioned the Senate for evidence of their appointments. Although he was a Quaker, Captain Harper also served under Washington, at Princeton, Monmouth, Brandywine, and Valley Forge. He commanded the artillery company at Washington's funeral in Alexandria. His father, John Harper, had been a major shipping merchant at Philadelphia, specializing in grain and flour, prior to his move to Alexandria early in the 1770s. John Harper prolifically demonstrated his Alexandria landholdings when he bequeathed a town lot to each of his twenty-nine children. In February 1801 one "Rus in Urbe" writing in the *Alexandria Gazette* urged the election of William Harper to the town council because he possessed "considerable property in Alexandria" and was therefore a man to be trusted. Shortly afterward, he was elected as an alderman. He died in 1829.

Whether these staunch Federalists really thought that the Supreme Court might somehow win them their commissions cannot be known. Perhaps they wanted, instead, to force the Supreme Court to speak out on the unconstitutionality of executive or legislative tampering with judicial offices. They may have intended only to give the Supreme Court an opportunity to lecture the President. Or they may even have had political ambitions which they thought this case would somehow serve. Whatever their intent, they must have been flabbergasted to see their Mandamus Case become the lever for invalidating a piece of *Federalist* legislation. Only the finely tuned political mind of John Marshall conceived this use for Federalists Marbury, Hooe, Ramsay, and Harper.

7

MR. MARBURY'S
DAY IN COURT

History has a way of occurring in obscure places, and in 1803 there were few places more obscure than the chambers of the United States Supreme Court. Up to this point in history the role of the Supreme Court had been so unmemorable that the planners of the new capital city simply forgot it. No chambers were provided for the Court, so that it was obliged to borrow a tiny room from the Senate. The clerk of the Senate was forced to relinquish his office to the third—obviously a distant third—branch of government. The Supreme Court continued to meet in this twenty-four by thirty-foot room, aptly dubbed the "cave of Trophonius" by John Randolph, until it was mercifully released when the British destroyed the Capitol in 1814. Then the Court moved into a private home for two years, which proved equally inadequate. From such beginnings, it is a tribute to John Marshall and his associates that the Supreme Court was soon able to gain so much prestige.

Marshall was such a major force in the Court's ascendance that there is a danger of overlooking his associates. Justice

Harold Burton insisted in 1955, however, that "we should see him as the leader of those able judges who constituted 'the Marshall Court.' Together, they made, nurtured, and protected great precedents." It is especially in the Federalist phase of the Marshall Court, when all his associates were legacies of George Washington and John Adams, that the others fade into the shadow of the lanky chief justice. Political realities and the personality of John Marshall were largely responsible for the preeminence which he so quickly acquired.

POLITICAL REALITIES

The Federalist party felt pushed to the wall by the election of 1800. Although its defeat then was hardly overwhelming, it is, nevertheless, a sobering experience for a political party to descend in a decade from the security of one-party rule to the insecurities of a two-party system and finally to the crushing blow of rejection at the polls. The one glimmer of hope was Federalist domination of the judiciary. If the Supreme Court was to be the salvation of Federalism, however, there must be no squabbling among the justices. Marshall immediately instituted the practice of having a majority opinion of the Court and preferably no dissenting opinions. This was a major factor in improving the Supreme Court's communication with the public and hence increasing its stature. Few persons whose livelihood did not depend on it had the patience to pursue the legal arguments of the justices through their seriatim (or individual) opinions. Under Marshall the *Court* spoke, rather than individual justices, and its voice was greatly magnified as a result. The fact that the justices were all members of a party which had become a harried minority made the cessation of seriatim opinions a matter of common political sense. Of the twenty-six decisions rendered by the Supreme Court during Jefferson's first administration, Marshall delivered the opinion in all but the two on which he did not sit, and no word of dissent was ever uttered by one of the Federalist justices.

Secretary of State Marshall had gained fame and some resentment from the manner in which he persuaded others in Adams' cabinet to adopt his views. His opportunities to assert his charm were even greater in the intimacy of the Supreme Court. Marshall persuaded all his associates to board with him at the same rooming house in Washington, D.C. As a result, issues broached in chambers would be settled around the fireplace at their joint home-away-from-home. This sociable arrangement, which continued long after the Republicans were in the majority on the Supreme Court, lessened the likelihood of disputes among the justices which might otherwise have shown up in dissenting opinions. This courtly camaraderie gave special influence to the judge with the most pleasing personality and the most logical mind, and Marshall was the possessor of both.

By present standards the Court before whom Charles Lee brought the appeal of the unfrocked justices of the peace was remarkably young. William Cushing was nearing seventy-one, and Samuel Chase would soon be sixty-one; but William Paterson was only fifty-seven, John Marshall and Alfred T. Moore were both forty-seven, and Bushrod Washington was only forty. Ironically, Moore would be the first to go, resigning in 1804; Paterson died in 1806, and Cushing and Chase followed in 1810 and 1811, leaving Marshall and Washington as the sole Federalist survivors.

MARSHALL ON THE BENCH

Chief Justice Marshall immmediately became a dominating figure on the Supreme Court. Yet there is truth in Robert Cushman's comment that "most readers of American history retain much more vivid impressions of Pocohontas than of the 'great Chief Justice.' " Judging from contemporary descriptions of Marshall in and out of court, he seems to have doffed many of his careless and awkward—indeed, sloppy—airs when he donned his judicial robes. Margaret Coit's description of the "tall, shambling John Marshall, with his rough hair and hearty laugh and the tumbled clothes that looked as if he had picked them out in some forgotten second-hand shop" is apparently a fair picture of Marshall off the bench. But in court he was a model of decorum. Most observers commented on his dignity, which surprised some of those who knew him personally.

The perceptive Joseph Story, who would be Marshall's disciple on the bench from 1810 until 1845, a decade after Marshall's death, gave the classic description of his future idol when he visited the Supreme Court five years after the *Marbury* decision:

> Marshall is of a tall, slender figure, not graceful nor imposing, but erect and steady. His hair is black, his eyes small and twinkling, his forehead rather low, but his features are in general harmonious. His manners are plain, yet dignified; and an unaffected modesty diffuses itself through all his actions. His dress is very simple, yet neat; his language chaste, but hardly elegant; it does not flow rapidly, but it seldom wants precision. In conversation he is quite familiar, but is occasionally embarrassed by a hesitancy and drawling. His thoughts are always clear and ingenious, sometimes striking, and not often inconclusive; he possesses great subtilty of mind, but it is only occasionally exhibited. I love his laugh,—it is too hearty for an intriguer,—and his good temper and unwearied patience are equally agreeable on the bench and in the study. His genius is, in my opinion, vigorous and powerful, less rapid than discriminating, and less vivid than uniform in its light. He examines the intricacies of a subject with calm and persevering circumspection, and unravels the mysteries with irresistible acuteness. He has not the majesty and compactness of thought of Dr. Johnson; but in subtle logic he is no unworthy disciple of David Hume.*

---

* Story to Samuel P. P. Fay, February 25, 1808, in William W. Story, ed., *Life and Letters of Joseph Story,* 2 vols. (Boston: Charles C. Little and James Brown, 1851), vol. I, pp. 166–167.

Story claimed to be "more phlegmatic than usual" in this letter, so "the approach is so much nearer the truth. Had I been in high spirits, you would probably have had the airy phantoms of fancy." After Story joined Marshall on the bench his references to the chief justice did, indeed, become much more flowery and idolatrous.

BUSHROD WASHINGTON

Marshall's closest associate on the Federalist Court was Bushrod Washington, whose reputation has especially suffered in the shadow of the chief justice. Washington was the favorite nephew of the revered George Washington, heir to Mount Vernon and the valuable historical documents which it contained, and the inspiration for Marshall's regrettably uninspired biography of the first President. Washington, like Marshall, was a charter member of Phi Beta Kappa at the College of William and Mary. (Another charter member was Spencer Roane, who later became the principal Jeffersonian pamphleteer against Marshall. This lifelong judicial and personal opponent of Marshall, it was generally assumed, would have been Thomas Jefferson's choice as chief justice if Adams and Marshall had not combined to fill the office early in 1801.) Later, Washington was a diligent legal student under James Wilson, whom he eventually succeeded on the Supreme Court.

John Adams was determined to appoint either John Marshall or Bushrod Washington to the Supreme Court in 1798; Marshall declined, leaving the way open for his college friend. Washington then served for thirty-one years, until 1829. He was an able lawyer and jurist, but he was so amenable to Marshall's leadership that he is one of the longest-lived "unknowns" in the history of the Supreme Court. Justice William Johnson, who was so often antagonized by Marshall's dominance, complained in 1822 that Marshall and Washington "are commonly estimated as one Judge."

Washington suffered, also, from a critical contemporary description which has become the basis of all historical sketches of him. George Ticknor saw him as "a little, sharp-faced gentleman with only one eye, and a profusion of snuff distributed over his face." A recent critic of the Marshall Court, Fred Rodell, builds from this outline to a peak of "Bushrodphobia" when he describes him as "sloppy, snuff-sniffing, slight of build and slight of mentality—whose chief qualification was obviously his name and who was to stick on the Court for thirty-one years, dully mouthing old Federalist doctrine to the very end."

When Joseph Story characterized the Supreme Court in 1808 he also remarked on Washington's short, boyish, unimpressive appearance, but significantly he added that Washington's "written opinions are composed with ability, and on the bench he exhibits great promptitude and firmness in decision. It requires intimacy to value him as he deserves." Washington's performance beyond the shadow of Marshall, in the circuit courts of the Middle Atlantic States, was so impressive that many years later Justice Lucius Q. C. Elmer of the New Jersey Supreme Court, described him in the most glowing terms: "If I was asked, who of all the judges you have known, do you consider to have been the best fitted for that high office, taking into the account integrity of character, learning, deportment, balance of mind, natural temper and disposition, and ability to ascertain and regard the true merits of a cause, as determined by the law that he was called to administer, I should say Bushrod Washington."

SAMUEL CHASE

The most striking member of the Marshall Court was the massive, white-haired Samuel Chase, whose broad, brownish-red face had given him the nickname "Bacon Face" among

Maryland lawyers. Since his arrival on the Supreme Court in 1796, Chase had been one of the most interesting—and most disliked—figures in American politics. His language was so forceful and his tone so assertive that his impeachment seemed inevitable if ever the Jeffersonians were to gain control of Congress. Chase's coarseness and partisanship both on and off the bench, especially in the handling of sedition cases in the waning months of the Adams administration, earned him the undying hostility of the Jeffersonians. Nor could they forget that Justice Chase openly campaigned for Adams in 1800. Even Joseph Story, who admired Chase, was a bit shocked at their first meeting. Chase seemed a "rough, but very sensible man" who was "irregular and sometimes ill-directed. . . . His manners are coarse, and in appearance harsh; but in reality he abounds with good humor." In 1807 Story thought him "the American Thurlow,—bold, impetuous, overbearing, and decisive." By 1808 he was "the living, I had almost said the exact, image of Samuel Johnson."

Never has so blatant a partisan sat on the Supreme Court. The fiercely Republican *Philadelphia Aurora* notified him early in 1801 that his "judicial" conduct was so inexcusable that "few men, perhaps, hold an humbler estimation among his fellow citizens." Yet Chase took a strangely roundabout route to achieve his reputation as the epitome of Federalist partisanship. He had been the most boisterous of Maryland revolutionaries beginning in 1765. First in his long career in the Maryland House of Burgesses and then in the First and Second Continental Congresses, he had always been a powerful advocate of American independence. He remained in Congress until 1778, serving on most of its significant committees. His speculative ventures during the war soon brought him to the attention of Alexander Hamilton, a young military officer soon destined to be the fiscal and philosophical genius of the Federalist party. In 1778 Hamilton published an attack on the "universally despised" Chase. "Were I inclined to make a satire upon the species," he said, "I would attempt a faithful description of your heart."

Chase's personally disastrous grain manipulations a decade later were less offensive to Hamilton, for by then Hamilton was overly sympathetic to the concerns of speculators. Chase did something even worse, though, from the Federalist standpoint. He opposed ratification of the United States Constitution, in both the Maryland convention and Maryland newspapers. As late as 1793 Chase continued to be loud—as he was in everything—in his condemnation of the British, for whom all Federalists had by then come to feel great tenderness. This checkered record has caused William W. Crosskey to overstate his case and deny that Chase even was a Federalist. Whatever he was when he was appointed in 1796, Chase was sufficiently Federalist by 1801 that John Adams eagerly sought to reward him by providing his son with a federal office; and the Republicans hated him more than any other man in America, with the possible exception of Chase's quondam critic Alexander Hamilton.

President Washington, who had exercised immense care in his appointments and who did not make a practice of appointing non-Federalists to office, knew of Chase's record. Perhaps it was mitigated by the feeling that anyone who had opposed the congressional and military intrigues against General George Washington as faithfully as Chase had during the Revolution could not be all bad. When the Republicans finally had the votes to impeach, and nearly to remove, Justice Chase in 1805, he was at last chastened, and his conduct in the circuit courts was vastly improved.

PATERSON, CUSHING, AND MOORE

William Paterson was a most unlikely candidate for a shadow or mere stooge of John Marshall. For many Federalists

Paterson was so obvious a choice as chief justice that they could only attribute the appointment of Marshall, instead, as proof of Adams' mental derangement. The scholarly justice came from a wealthy family which had a natural home in the Federalist party. Paterson had waged a bitter struggle against future Federalist leaders in the Constitutional Convention of 1787, when he opposed the nationalistic ventures of Hamilton, King, Wilson, Washington, and the Morrises. Once he had succeeded in his efforts to protect the "small" states, however, he became New Jersey's greatest supporter of the Constitution and a lifelong Federalist. Although a fellow delegate described Paterson's physical appearance as unimpressive in the convention, he was "a Classic, a Lawyer, and an Orator" whose abilities "create wonder and astonishment."

Like so many other supporters of the Constitution, Paterson was rewarded by election to the United States Senate. Before leaving to become governor of New Jersey, he participated significantly in the writing of the Judiciary Act of 1789. The first nine sections appear to have been largely his work. Unlike Marshall, who managed both at once, Paterson's political career briefly delayed his judicial career. Washington appointed him to the Supreme Court on February 27, 1793, when a few days of the Senate term to which Paterson was elected still remained. The President overlooked the constitutional barrier against appointing a senator to an office created during his legislative term because Paterson had left the Senate three years before his term ended. Washington withdrew Paterson's name on February 28 and resubmitted it as soon as it was legal—on March 4. Paterson was then confirmed by the Senate almost immediately.

William Cushing was nearing the end of a judicial career that spanned a half-century, twenty-nine years in Massachusetts and twenty-one years on the Supreme Court. Only Oliver Wendell Holmes has equaled this record, and he had to serve until ninety-one to do it. Cushing was not only the oldest justice with the longest service among Marshall's associates; he was the *first* associate justice appointed by Washington. His judicial opinions set no records, however. The modest and affable Cushing wrote only brief opinions, concurring with the majority, even during the decade of seriatim decisions. Naturally, he found Marshall's advocacy of Court opinions delivered by Marshall much to his liking. Aside from being the first associate justice and the first to continue to serve on the Supreme Court after the onset of senility, Cushing was most notable as the last American judge to wear the full English judicial wig (which he abandoned when he found it attracted crowds in New York where the Supreme Court first convened) and for his historic ruling in 1783 that slavery in Massachusetts was outlawed by the state constitution. Cushing was a member of the convention that adopted the Massachusetts constitution in 1780, and he was vice-chairman of the Massachusetts convention of 1788, which ratified the United States Constitution.

The junior member of the Court, with the exception of the Chief Justice himself, was Alfred T. Moore, whose career was so brief that he left no mark on the Supreme Court. Moore was appointed in 1799 and resigned in 1804 because of ill health. He had a brilliant legal career, highlighted by service as attorney general of North Carolina from 1782 to 1791; he served with distinction in the Revolution, yet still favored leniency toward Loyalists who wanted to return to North Carolina; he supported the United States Constitution; and, most important, he was a good Federalist in a state where Federalists were a rarity.

DEMAND FOR A WRIT OF MANDAMUS

The case of *Marbury* v. *Madison* first came before this group of Supreme Court justices on December 21, 1801, when Charles Lee appeared to seek a writ of mandamus to command Secretary of State Madison to deliver the elusive commissions to the aspiring justices, Marbury, Hooe, Ramsay, and Harper. Attorney General Levi Lincoln, who as acting secretary of state had done whatever was done with the commissions, appeared only to say that he had nothing to say. Only the pugnacious Chase was prepared to rule immediately on the case. Marshall instead issued a routine order the next day—if any command to a cabinet member can truly be routine—that Madison show cause why a writ of mandamus should not be issued against him. The question was scheduled for further argument early in the next term; it was presumed then that this meant August of 1802 rather than February of 1803. This long cooling-off period may have been fortunate for the Supreme Court, for the ease with which Congress could toy with the sessions of the judiciary may have been a timely reminder of the limits of judicial power and prevented a reckless, and perhaps fatal, test of strength by the Court.

James Madison simply ignored the order, and the *Philadelphia Aurora* was confident that Federalist talk of "dragging the president before the court and impeaching him, and a wonderful deal of similar nothingness" would prove to be only "*fume* which can excite no more than a ludic[r]ous irritation." Congress, however, did not take the rule so lightly. Senator John Breckenridge of Kentucky, for instance, thought it a "bold stroke against the Executive authority of the Government." He did not expect the matter to be pursued but, even so, "the consequences of invading the Executive in this manner are deemed here a high-handed exertion of Judiciary power." Representative John Randolph warned that the "inquisitorial" judges would rule both the executive and the legislature if Congress failed to discipline them.

When Madison ignored the Court's ruling, Lee and his clients had to seek means of proving to the Supreme Court, including the chief justice who had once mishandled their commissions, that they actually had been appointed to office. As if to remind the Senate that the "Mandamus Case" would

soon be heard, Marbury, Hooe, and Ramsay petitioned the
Senate on the eve of the February 1803 term of the Supreme
Court to permit copies of Senate action on their appointments
to be taken from the Senate executive journal. Its sponsor in
the Senate thought the request so reasonable, that he was
confident "it would pass without objection." Naturally, the
Republican majority would not countenance any such inva-
sion of what they called Senate and executive privacy! Robert
Wright of Maryland was typical in his rejection of an "auda-
cious attempt to pry into Executive secrets, by a tribunal
which had no authority to do any such thing."

A MOST UNUSUAL "TRIAL"

The *Marbury* trial, which began on February 9, 1803, would
be a fitting subject for a comic opera. Gilbert and Sullivan,
who gibed so effectively at British bar and bench, would have
had especially great fun with it. To begin with, a prime
"villain" in the piece was the presiding officer. John Marshall
had forged this chain of undelivered commissions by his failure to deliver them. Marshall admitted especially regretting
the withholding of the commissions because "I fear some
blame may be imputed to me," so surely no one would have
disputed a decision not to participate in this case because of
personal involvement; many have criticized his judgment in
deciding instead to participate. It is possible that three associate justices did not participate in the decision. Cushing
appears from the minutes to have been absent throughout the
trial and the decision. Paterson may have missed the first day
of testimony and Moore the second. In the unlikely event that
none of these participated in the decision, Secretary of State-
Chief Justice Marshall's vote would then have counted for
one-third rather than only one-sixth.

It can even be questioned whether there really was a *Marbury* trial rather than a mere inquest. James Madison does

not seem to have paid the slightest attention to "his" case, and Attorney General Levi Lincoln was present merely as an observer and sometime witness. Thus Charles Lee's case for Marbury was uncontested. The Supreme Court has kept no file of this landmark case, so our only knowledge of it comes from the unofficial report of Midnight Judge William Cranch, who served as a volunteer court reporter, and from various newspaper accounts.

The decision is renowned as a successful political coup for Marshall and the Supreme Court, even though Madison (and thus Jefferson) was technically the victor. Marshall lectured the Jefferson administration at great length about the necessity for restraints on government, in language that can best be described as Jeffersonian. However, he concluded that, because the law which authorized the Court to issue a writ of mandamus in such a case was unconstitutional, the Court lacked jurisdiction to hear the case about which it had said so much. This backward approach to the case justifies the claims of Marshall-*Marbury* critics (including the Supreme Court in 1926) that the references to the Chief Executive and his power of appointment and removal are utterly extraneous and therefore obiter dictum. Some have argued, with much less legitimacy, that the entire decision, including the voiding of federal legislation, was obiter dictum and therefore no precedent.

Finally, this milestone in the history of judicial review came as a complete surprise to everyone outside the circle of Marshall's fireside. It was not the exercise of judicial review, but its exercise in the *Marbury* case which was astonishing. Boudin suggests that it was "dragged in by the hair, so to speak, by Marshall himself, for purely political considerations." In 1802 and 1803 congressmen of both parties discussed the likelihood of such action by the Supreme Court at great length. It was widely assumed that the Court might dare such a venture in *Stuart* v. *Laird,* voiding the Republican repeal of the Judiciary Act of 1801. Instead, the Supreme Court chose the safer course of confining its assertion of judicial review of national laws to the *Marbury* case, where it was meaningless except as a precedent, and then upholding the judiciary repeal a week later in the potentially explosive *Stuart* case. The Republican press was so delighted by the Jeffersonian victories in these two cases that it did not recognize that William Marbury had been used as a tool to plant the seeds of judicial review.

James Madison's relation to Marbury and to Marshall adds further irony. Madison did not assume office until May 2, when he was sworn in by John Adams' son-in-law and Midnight Judge William Cranch, so he probably never even saw the commissions for which he was being sued. The Republican congressman who surmised that "they were disposed of with the other waste paper and rubbish of the office" early in March was most likely correct. At any rate, there has been no sign of them in the 170 years since they were first left on John Marshall's desk. Madison appears to have been as unconcerned about the case as he was uninvolved in its origin. If his surviving papers are a true indication, he was so preoccupied with the French acquisition of New Orleans that he simply ignored the judiciary and the case in which he was a supposed protagonist.

Madison was neither Marbury's tyrant nor Marshall's enemy. Yet Madison had more personal reason to dislike Marshall than Jefferson ever had. In Mason v. Wilson, 1 Cranch 45 (1801), Marshall upheld the legal arguments of Joseph H. Daveiss that 30,000 acres of Kentucky land bought long before by George Mason, William Moore, and James Madison, Sr. (the Grandfather of the Constitution) rightfully belonged to George Wilson because of a technicality, despite the highly questionable nature of Wilson's claim. The fact that Daveiss informed Secretary of State Madison shortly before the case went to court that the Wilson claim was by then actually Daveiss' own and that Daveiss married Marshall's sister in

1803, would have earned Marshall the undying enmity of a less equable man than James Madison. Yet while the President continued to nurse his animosity for the chief justice, Secretary of State Madison welcomed Marshall as a dinner guest. Contemporaries report that there was good personal feeling between Marshall and Madison even in 1812, when Marshall was extremely critical of "Mr. Madison's War" and was widely regarded as a possible Federalist opponent to Madison's reelection. As they aged, each continued to speak highly of the other.

Madison even had kind words for Marshall's *Life of Washington,* a big gray book which was a red flag to Jefferson. Madison thought it "highly respectable, as a specimen of historical composition, much more so than the critics have generally been inclined to allow." He added, however, that the fifth volume, which covered the birth of the Republican party, was "quite inaccurate and ill-digested" and the "bias of party feeling is obvious." He was sure that "Judge Marshall would write differently at the present day [1827] and with his present impressions."

THE CALLING OF WITNESSES

Barred by propriety from summoning the one witness who could best testify to the signing and sealing of the missing documents—his old friend John Marshall—Charles Lee turned to many other officials in his search for evidence. Before the trial, unavailing appeals were made to Madison, to his clerks in the State Department, to the secretary of the Senate, and finally to the Senate itself. All that was learned was that the commissions—if such there were!—were not in the State Department files. Summoned to testify before the Supreme Court were Attorney General Levi Lincoln, Judge James Marshall, and two holdover State Department clerks.

Chief Clerk Jacob Wagner and Daniel Brent, Federalist remnants from before Marshall's days in the State Department, strongly objected to appearing before the Supreme Court, contending that they were "not bound to disclose any facts relating to the business or transactions" of the State Department. Lee argued at length, however, that while the secretary of state is accountable only to the President when acting as his agent, when he performs public ministerial duties he is "an independent and an accountable officer" and therefore "compellable by mandamus to do his duty." The recording and preserving of nonconfidential records, such as commissions of justices of the peace, are duties "of a public kind, and his clerks can have no exclusive privileges" to remain silent. Throughout his brief, Lee sought to blunt the horns of Marshall's dilemma by minimizing the conflict with the executive department. The President would not, and could not, be coerced; a mandamus cannot go "to the president in any case" nor to the secretary of state "in all cases." But here it was James Madison the record keeper, not James Madison the Number Two man in the Jefferson administration, who was at fault.

The Supreme Court ordered Wagner and Brent to be sworn and to give written answers, though it recognized their right to state objections to questions which they felt were improper to answer. Both proved to have pretty bad memories, probably because they had pretty good jobs, and they wanted to keep them. Wagner remained chief clerk until 1807, when he resigned to edit a Baltimore Federalist newspaper whose principal target was James Madison. Brent was still in the State Department in 1837, when Madison, Marshall, and Marbury were all dead.

Chief Clerk Wagner was still in office largely because Marshall had urged him to remain and because Madison recognized that he was a valuable, though Federalist, asset to the State Department. Shortly after Madison asked him to continue as chief clerk, Wagner wrote to Timothy Pickering, the Federalist secretary of state who had appointed him, that he had intended to "rid myself from a situation subject to vicis-situdes" until persuaded by Marshall to remain "on public grounds." Then he "easily fled into a consent to remain on honorable terms." His testimony lived up to his pledge to Madison of "neutrality of conduct." "At this distance of time he could not recollect whether he had seen any commission" for the applicants, though he did recall telling Marbury and Ramsay that two of the commissions in question were signed and another was not. This he learned from someone whom he declined, and was not required, to identify. Wagner also thought that some of the commissions were recorded, but he did not know whether these included the commissions of the applicants, "as he had not had recourse to the book for more than twelve months past." He was not directed to refresh his memory by reexamining the records.

Utilizing a strangely selective memory, Daniel Brent, "did not remember certainly" the names of any of the individuals whose commissions were signed by President Adams, but he was "almost certain" that commissions were made out for Hooe and Marbury and that Ramsay was omitted by mistake. He personally carried the commissions to Adams for his signa-ture and then back to the State Department where the Great Seal of the United States was affixed. He thought none of the signed and sealed commissions were recorded and that none were "sent out, or delivered" to the intended recipients. "He did not know what became of them, nor did he know that they are now in the office of the Secretary of State." Two days be-fore the *Marbury* decision was rendered, Lee produced the affidavit of a former State Department clerk who recalled that Adams had signed commissions for both Hooe and Marbury.

Attorney General Levi Lincoln, who had been acting secre-tary of state and who presumably did whatever was done with the commissions, was only a slightly more willing witness. He was torn by his respect for "the jurisdiction of this court" and for "the rights of the executive." Lest he inadvertently "dis-

close his official transactions while acting as Secretary of State"
or "answer any thing which might tend to criminate himself"
he asked that the questions be submitted in writing and that
he be given until the next day to answer them. Cranch's report
of the case states that the delay was intended to permit him
"to consider of his answers," but the *Philadelphia Aurora*
attributes it to the necessity of his attending the "committee
on the Georgia claims." As James Madison and Treasury
Secretary Albert Gallatin were the other members of the committee attempting to untangle the Yazoo land mess, Lincoln
and Madison may well have conferred regarding the answers
which Lincoln would make. The judges, speaking seriatim
for a change, granted Lincoln an evening's thinking-time, but
"they had no doubt he ought to answer" because "the fact
whether such commissions had been in the office or not, could
not be a confidential fact; it is a fact which all the world have
a right to know."

The next day, February 10, Lincoln answered all but the
key question; "What has been done with the commissions?"
He recalled that he had seen a number of signed and sealed
commissions, though he did not recall whether there were any
for Hooe, Marbury, or Ramsay. He did not believe that any
had been sent to the appointees. When he was directed by
President Jefferson to prepare general commissions, one each
for Washington County and Alexandria County, he regarded
this as superseding the Adams-Marshall commissions. "He had
no hesitation in saying that he did not know that [the Adams-
Marshall commissions] ever came to the possession of Mr.
Madison, nor did he know that they were in the office when
Mr. Madison took possession of it." He asked that he be
required to say no more about the disposition of the commissions. Unfortunately for curious historians, the Court honored
this request, for "if they never came to the possession of Mr.
Madison, it was immaterial to the present cause what had been
done with them by others." The *Washington Federalist* chided

"this great man" who, when "sworn in the usual manner, was asked a simple question, but could not answer it till they gave it to him in writing, and he went off and spent a whole day and night ... with closed doors; and then he made out to remember that he had forgot all about it."

LEE'S THREE QUESTIONS

Having "proved the existence of the commissions," Lee turned to the key question, whether the Supreme Court could do anything about it. He approached this by answering three rhetorical questions:

"1st.   Whether the Supreme Court can award the writ of mandamus in any case?

"2nd.   Whether it will lie to a Secretary of State in any case whatever?

"3rd.   Whether, in the present case, the court may award a mandamus to James Madison, secretary of state?"

Answering the first was easy. "By reason of its supremacy," the Supreme Court simply must have "the superintendence of the inferior tribunals and officers, whether judicial or ministerial." According to Anglo-American legal tradition, "every right, when withheld, must have a remedy, and every injury, its proper redress." Some injuries can only be redressed by a writ of mandamus, so such a power must exist—and where else but "in that court which the constitution and laws have made supreme, and to which they have given appellate jurisdiction?"

If English tradition and constitutional implication were not sufficiently persuasive, Congress had specifically granted such authority to the Supreme Court. Section 13 of the Judiciary Act of 1789, effective again after the repeal of the 1801 act, provided that the Supreme Court could issue "writs of mandamus, in cases warranted by the principles and usages of law, to any courts appointed, or persons holding office, under the authority of the United States." Lee anticipated, and attempted to undercut, Marshall's later argument against the constitutionality of Section 13 by asserting that Congress "is not restrained from conferring original jurisdiction in other cases than those mentioned in the constitution." Lee cited a number of earlier cases in which mandamus was sought against government officials; although the writ was not granted in these cases, the power to issue it had never been questioned. Hence legislative construction and judicial practice were agreed regarding the legitimacy of a writ of mandamus in such a case.

The second question, whether a secretary of state could be issued such a writ, was more political and therefore more explosive. Lee denied that such an action was in any way comparable to ordering about the President. Mandamus or any other judicial action would be off-limits for the President, who could be disciplined only by impeachment. The same would be true of the secretary of state when he is acting as the agent of the President. But as "a recorder of the laws of the United States, as keeper of the great seal, as recorder of deeds of lands, of letters patent, and of commissions, &c., he is a ministerial officer of the people of the United States" and, as such, within the reach of the courts. "It is true he is a high officer, but he is not above law." If there is *any* mandamus power, Lee contended that it must extend to the secretary of state. Justice Paterson asked if it is the duty of the secretary of state to deliver commissions unless 'expressly directed not to by the President. Lee replied that after signing a commission the President "has done with it," and after it is sealed by the secretary of state the appointment is completed. A secretary of state who then refuses to deliver the commission "does wrong."

Finally, Lee considered the question of whether a writ of mandamus ought to be issued to James Madison, the specific secretary of state involved in this case. Lee argued that a justice of the peace is a judicial officer appointed for five years and, therefore, not removable by the President. While admitting that the income and dignity which might be derived from this office were small, Lee insisted that the case was not trivial. No less a principle than judicial independence was at stake. He claimed that the citizens of the District of Columbia were fearful of such high-handed tampering by the secretary of state with their judiciary. He concluded that in this case mandamus is not only a proper remedy, but an absolute obligation of the Supreme Court. "If the applicant makes out a proper case, the court are bound to grant it. They can refuse justice to no man."

The justices may have been a bit embarrassed by the absence of any reply to Lee. When Attorney General Levi Lincoln refused to make any response, the Court then asked if there was "any other gentleman of the bar who might *wish* to offer any observations." When this entreaty was met with silence the Court "postponed their decision to a future day."

8

MARSHALL RAMPANT, MADISON REBUKED, MARBURY REBUFFED

John Marshall's first major decision provided a fitting climax to the Marbury trial. In its own quietly judicial and tediously verbose way, the decision was as unusual as the comic opera proceedings of the trial. Marshall adroitly teetered between the political sin of bowing to Jeffersonian Republicanism and the personal catastrophe of giving Jefferson grounds for impeaching or, perhaps worse, ignoring him and the Supreme Court. It seemed that any step Marshall might take would hurt both himself and the Federalist party. If he ordered delivery of Marbury's commission as a justice of the peace, Jefferson and Madison would simply ignore him, and the foundation of judicial power would become quicksand. Andrew Jackson's famous (and probably apocryphal) snub of the judiciary in 1832, "John Marshall has made his decision:—now let him enforce it!" might instead have been attributed to Jefferson. The year 1803 was a more dangerous time than 1832 for the judiciary to demonstrate its weakness: for it had never yet shown that it had much strength. A ruling against

Marbury would have been regarded as a vindication of the dismissal of Federalist officeholders and, by implication, the Republican repeal of the Judiciary Act of 1801. It seemed so obvious that Jefferson must triumph over Marshall in this case, whatever the decision, that a historical novelist would be tempted to portray Marbury and company as Republicans who had infiltrated the Federalist party just for this nefarious purpose.

By blithely rearranging the principal issues of the case, thus enabling him to delay a ruling of nonjurisdiction until the last moment, Marshall salvaged the best of both bad situations. He ruled that Marbury was entitled to his commission and lectured the President for depriving him of his rights. After this partisan lecture, however, Marshall concluded that, even though Marbury's rights had been violated and mandamus was the proper remedy, Marbury had come to the wrong place to seek redress. The Supreme Court had no jurisdiction to act in this case, and Section 13 of the Judiciary Act of 1789, by which the Federalist Congress had attempted to grant such jurisdiction, was therefore void. Thus the daring and partisan John Marshall lambasted the President and established an important precedent for the review of federal legislation by the Supreme Court, while the circumspect and restrained John Marshall decided the case for Jefferson and Madison.

CHARACTERISTICS OF MARSHALL'S DECISIONS

It was here that Marshall introduced his practice of using language that outraged Jeffersonians while arriving at a decision which would please them. Two decades later, Jefferson was still protesting the Marshall decisions' nationalistic or mercantilistic language which went beyond the scope of the immediate cases. As the final decision of the Supreme Court was that it lacked jurisdiction to hear Marbury's appeal, everything which preceded the consideration of jurisdiction has generally been regarded as impertinent, hence obiter dictum. No less an authority than Justice Samuel F. Miller wrote that "much of the decision was in many respects obiter dictum because the court declared in the end that they had no jurisdiction in the case." In 1926 Chief Justice William Howard Taft ruled that Marshall's lecture on the President's power of removal was only an obiter dissertation. It was Marshall's eagerness to go beyond the immediate case, even at the risk of impertinence, which enabled him to create major state papers from trivial cases—including Marbury's. This readiness to transcend the limits of a moot or feigned case caused his major biographer, Albert J. Beveridge, to raise him above mere interpreters of the law and rank him with "Moses and other mighty law-givers of the world."

Marshall's first important decision characterizes his entire judicial career in many other ways. One characteristic was the speed with which so lengthy a decision (or the length at which so speedy a decision) was prepared. In *Marbury,* as in *McCulloch* v. *Maryland,* one must suspect that Marshall was working on his decision well before the issues were presented in court. Less than two weeks after the trial, Marshall turned out a decision of more than 11,000 words and won the unanimous support of the associate justices. This was merely a warm-up for the speed record which he would set in March 1819 when he delivered the great, though shorter, *McCulloch* v. *Maryland* decision only three days after counsel had ended debate.

Marshall is justly famed for his directness and great capacity for condensing constitutional issues into a succinct statement; yet he is likewise noted (or notorious) for tedious and verbose reiteration. The *Marbury* decision demonstrates both of these characteristics, though the latter is more evident. Nearly 8,500 words (118 paragraphs) had been read before Marshall finally began his exposition of judicial review. From this point he presented a succinct restatement of the arguments for judicial review which had been so prevalent in Congress the preceding winter, when the Federalists urged the Supreme Court to prevent the Republicans from voiding the Judiciary Act of 1801.

Marshall's performance in this first significant decision lived up to Francis W. Gilmer's feathery description of him. Gilmer admired the reasoned eloquence of John Marshall as a lawyer, but he was struck by Marshall's difficulties at the outset of an argument, when he spoke "with reluctance, hesitation, and vacancy of eye." Gilmer had likened Marshall at this stage to "some great bird, which flounders and flounces on the earth for a while before it acquires the impetus to sustain its soaring flight."

Marshall was as conscious as his listeners of his tendency toward verbosity. In fact, he apologized at the end of Gibbons v. Ogden, 9 Wheaton 1 (1824), for consuming so much time in "the attempt to demonstrate propositions which may have been thought axioms. It is felt that the tediousness inseparable from the endeavor to prove that which is already clear, is imputable to a considerable part of this opinion." He recognized this flaw while writing the *Gibbons* decision, even before he had the benefit of a fidgeting audience. Thus he could still have pruned it in chambers, but Marshall felt that the decision depended "on a chain of principles which it was necessary to preserve unbroken" even if some of the links were "nearly self-evident." In the introduction to *Marbury* v. *Madison* he explained that so complete an exposition was required by the "peculiar delicacy of this case, the novelty of some of its circumstances, and the real difficulty attending the points which occur in it."

Often, lengthy judicial decisions are padded with extensive borrowings from other judges, but this was not John Marshall's way, nor was it common among his contemporaries. Marshall is said to have turned frequently to Justice Joseph Story to ask for the legal precedents to justify Marshall's commonsense decisions. If this really did occur, at least it did not occur in his great decisions, for not a single precedent was cited in *McCulloch* v. *Maryland* (1819), Cohens v. Virginia, 6 Wheaton 264 (1821), Dartmouth College v. Woodward, 4 Wheaton 518 (1819), and Sturges v. Crowninshield, 4 Wheaton 122 (1819). The Marshall pattern of scanty documentation was established in *Marbury* v. *Madison*. He cited no judicial authority on the crucial issue of judicial review, even though he certainly was aware of some. Nor did he base his philosophy of judicial review on anything within the Constitution or on any reputed attitude of the delegates who wrote or ratified the Constitution. Characteristically, he found it unnecessary to rationalize judicial review historically, because the power was implicit in nearly all written constitutions, and certainly in the Constitution of the United States. The only legal precedent cited in the lengthy *Marbury* opinion is an English decision on the usage of the writ of mandamus, though he adds that "many others were relied on" in his study of mandamus. When Marshall argued from the other side of the bench, he had also relied on logic and common sense rather than judicial authority; most of the Marshall arguments which have survived in the *Virginia Reports* offer no judicial precedents.

Despite its length, *Marbury* v. *Madison* is not stuffed with the flowery effusions so characteristic of the oratory of that time. The down-to-earth tone of this opinion is characteristic both of Marshall's career at the Virginia bar before he came to national prominence and of his later decisions. Virginia contemporaries were astonished at Marshall's ability to make his point and win his cases without rhetorical flourishes. "There is no stopping to weave garlands of flowers," remarked that great legal garland maker William Wirt, as he launched into a tribute to Marshall's skill as a lawyer. Even "without the aid of fancy, without the advantages of person, voice, attitude, gesture, or any of the ornaments of an orator," Marshall was to Wirt "one of the most eloquent men in the world" because he seized his listeners' attention "with irresistible force" and never let go until they were convinced. Benjamin H. Latrobe wrote that as a lawyer Marshall's inferiority "in voice and manner" was offset by his genius for driving to the heart of every issue: "He speaks like a man of plain common sense, while he delights and informs the most acute." Francis Gilmer was still unimpressed with Marshall's *style* even when he had attained his eventual "unbroken stream of eloquence." Marshall's incapacity for oratory and his genius for logic are ably summed up in Gilmer's contrast of Marshall and Edmund Randolph at the bar. "In Mr. Marshall's speech all is reasoning; in Mr. Randolph's every thing is declamation. One is awkward; the other graceful. One is indifferent as to words, and slovenly in his pronunciation; the other adapts his phrases to the sense with poetic felicity; his voice to the sound with musical exactness. There is no breach in the train of Mr. Marshall's thoughts; little connexion between Mr. Randolph's."

A more recent commentator, Benjamin W. Palmer, has aptly described Marshall's language, however repetitive, as "muscular, unembellished, unadorned. It was mind working, clarity of thought, precision of logic, unscreened by decoration or rhetoric." To Palmer, Marshall's words were "athletes stripped for action" which ran "swiftly to the goal of his conclusion and desire." Thomas Jefferson was equally impressed with Marshall's talents for persuasion, according to Joseph Story. In 1843, Story informed his law classes at Harvard that Jefferson had once declared that:

> When conversing with Marshall I never admit anything. So sure as you admit any position to be good, no matter how remote from the conclusion he seeks to establish, you are gone. So great is his sophistry you must never give him an affirmative answer or you will be forced to grant his conclusion. Why, if he were to ask me if it were daylight or not, I'd reply, "Sir, I don't know, I can't tell."*

* Charles Richard Williams, *The Life of Rutherford Birchard Hayes*, 2 vols. (Boston: Houghton Mifflin Company, 1914), vol. I, p. 33.

The quiet judiciousness for which Marshall was known in his military and political life was characteristic of the Marshall Court as well—no matter how big a bomb he was setting under Jefferson or his states' rights disciples. His gentleness, calmness, and judiciousness are commented on by most observers of the Marshall Court, even those who hated the decisions which he announced so matter-of-factly. Albert J. Beveridge, a friendly biographer, praises his "patience, consideration, and prudence" and "the gentleness of his voice and manner" in the Burr trial; Claude G. Bowers, whose pen was in the service of Jefferson, sneered that Marshall was "suave, almost unctuous, wearing a mask of impartial benevolence" in the Burr trial. While they disputed his motives, both agreed that Marshall at least *appeared* impartial in a case in which political prejudice was hard to avoid. Contemporary descriptions of Marshall's conduct in *Marbury* v. *Madison,* an equally explosive political case, have not survived. Almost surely, though, he used the same low but persuasive voice, the same quiet judiciousness which would characterize him on the bench for three more decades. Although Marshall's manner on the bench was invariably one of good humor, neither wit nor humor had any place in his written decisions. As Story put it, Marshall believed that "judges ought to be more learned than witty." Marshall's decisions are much more solemn than Marshall himself was.

Marshall was the very image of sweet reason as he searched "anxiously" for any justification for withholding Marbury's commission. To show his good faith he first exploded "a supposition by no means unquestionable" and then a position "barely possible" before concluding that justice was entirely on Marbury's side. He likewise found investigation of the acts of the secretary of state "peculiarly irksome, as well as delicate," because of that officer's relationship with the President. Marshall piously protested that it was "scarcely necessary" for the Supreme Court to point out that it would never meddle with the prerogatives of the executive. It was "absurd and excessive" to think that the Supreme Court would intrude in "questions in their nature political or which are by the constitution and laws, submitted to the executive." Twenty-one years later, in Osborne v. The Bank of the United States, 9 Wheaton 738 (1824), Marshall primly declared that "Courts are the mere instruments of the law, and can will nothing." This retreat from policy-making was more apparent than real, for Marshall demonstrated in the *Marbury* opinion and many others that the Supreme Court would decide which "nonpolitical" questions it could hear and which "political" questions it must turn away.

Still another respect in which *Marbury* v. *Madison* was characteristic of all Marshall decisions was the fact that the Court spoke as one, with John Marshall providing both the guiding genius and the vocal cords. He became the spokesman of the Supreme Court on August 11, 1801, with the first opinion rendered after he became chief justice, and he never relinquished this role until his death. *Marbury* v. *Madison* was the first of thirty-six constitutional decisions which Marshall would present for the Supreme Court. He wrote the decision in every case over which he presided during the period of Federalist monopoly, and in only one instance was there even a separate concurring opinion. Marshall's dominance lessened as Jefferson appointees began to appear, but still he wrote and delivered the vast majority of opinions.

Unfortunately, surviving records do not show how Marshall went about destroying the tradition of opinions delivered seriatim (or individually) by each justice. Probably the other justices were political realists enough to see that, if they were to be the last hope of Federalism, they could not afford the luxury of publicizing their internal squabbles through separate decisions. To the end of his days, Jefferson was haunted by the specter of the judiciary "cooking up opinions in conclave." Less than a year before his death, Jefferson tried to organize a campaign to restore seriatim decisions.

POLITICAL REALITIES OF
MARBURY V. *MADISON*

Politics were not far from Marshall's mind as he composed the *Marbury* v. *Madison* decision. The most frequently borrowed description of the opinion is Edward S. Corwin's judgment that it was "a deliberate partisan coup." He thought it smelled "strongly of powder, for the battle between the chief justice and President Jefferson was already on." To Louis Boudin the opinion was "a political pamphlet, a campaign document in the then pending struggle between the Federalists and Anti-Federalists." President Martin Van Buren attributed the tone of *Marbury* v. *Madison* to the fact that Marshall "had been snatched from the political caldron, heated to redness by human passions, almost at the moment of his first appearance on the bench." Van Buren's prose is too fiery, though he is nearer the truth than Marshall disciples who regard the Chief Justice as a model of judicial impartiality.

A worthwhile exercise for those who rationalize Marshall's political decisions would be to rearrange *Marbury* v. *Madison* hypothetically and try to determine if the opinion would have been the same if the Court were considering the action of a Federalist President. The lengthy lecture to the President on his obligation to protect the rights of individuals, even persons of a different political persuasion, was not essential to the decision. Would Marshall have persisted in this gratuitous slap at a coequal branch of the government if the President had been John Adams rather than Thomas Jefferson? Surely not. The decision that William Marbury was not entitled to his commission could have been reached without introducing judicial review. Would Marshall have found it so essential to assert judicial power in 1803 if the executive and legislature had been safely Federalist rather than dangerously Republican? Probably, he would still have wanted to establish the precedent for judicial review of federal legislation. To carry this hypothetical rearrangement of history to its political extreme, would Marshall have asserted judicial power in the face of a Federalist Congress and President if his brethren of the court had somehow been, let us say, Thomas Jefferson, William Johnson, James Madison, Andrew Jackson, John Breckenridge, and Spencer Roane? Surely not.

Political realities helped to dictate the *Marbury* decision. Thomas Jefferson's grasp on the other branches of government tightened with each succeeding election, and the Federalist judiciary could expect to find itself increasingly more isolated. Jefferson had spoken softly about the Federalists in his inaugural address, but he was obviously offended by Federalist dominance of a branch of government which was beyond the voter's reach. Rather than wait for Jefferson to take the initiative in his quarrel with the Supreme Court, Marshall used the uncommissioned justices of the peace to make his case for judicial power.

The *Marbury* decision was an example of "good Federalism" in 1803. But in two respects it was a violation of what had been basic Federalism until the Federalists fell from power in 1801. An extremely powerful executive and broad construction of the Constitution were both basic to Hamiltonian Federalism.

1. Although this opinion is best known for its assertion of judicial review of federal legislation, the Supreme Court reviewed the executive as well when it decided to rule on who could and who could not be removed by the President. Both President and Congress must be bound by judicial decisions if the United States was to be "a government of laws." The legislative review has caught the attention of historians, but it was the Court's tampering with executive authorities which excited Marshall's contemporaries. Presidential dominance in executive matters such as appointments had been a Federalist article of faith so long as the Presidents themselves had been Federalists. Alexander Hamilton's theory of executive leadership was so expansive that James Madison quite justifiably

accused him of looking to the British royal prerogative for
inspiration rather than to the United States Constitution.
Later courts have enthusiastically accepted the *Marbury* doctrine of judicial review of legislation, but judicial review of
the President's appointments and removals has been a different
matter. On this issue, they have sided with the Hamilton Federalism of the 1790s rather than the Marshall Federalism of
1803. In 1897 the Supreme Court ruled that, when the statute
is silent as to removal of an officer, the President can remove
him at will. In 1926 it upheld the President's authority to
remove even an officer who was appointed for a fixed term. In
Myers v. United States, 272 U.S. 52 (1926), the Taft Court
failed to overrule the *Marbury* limitations on the President's
removal power only because this was regarded as obiter dictum
and therefore no precedent.

2. The strict construction of the Constitution which Marshall used in *Marbury* v. *Madison* was not only out of step
with Hamilton's Federalism of the 1790s, but also with Marshall's Federalism from 1804 to 1835. The clause of the Con-
·stitution that Marshall used to justify voiding Section 13 of
the Judiciary Act of 1789 could as well have been read so that
it upheld the constitutionality of the legislation. Instead, Marshall gave it the narrowest possible reading. It is ironic that
the master of broad construction should be best known for a
decision which is so completely out of character. Answering
the claim in *Gibbons* v. *Ogden* (1824) that the Constitution
should be construed strictly, Marshall argued: "We cannot
perceive the propriety of this strict construction, nor adopt it
as a rule by which the Constitution is to be expounded." That
was the *real* John Marshall, the Marshall who Jefferson claimed
had converted the Supreme Court into an "engine of consolidation" which would eventually destroy the United States.
Only a year after *Marbury* v. *Madison,* in a case lacking its
political overtones, Marshall went out of his way to justify the
broad construction of the Constitution which was so typical

of him and Federalism. United States v. Fisher, 2 Cranch 358 (1804), contained the seeds of the broad construction which Marshall would expound so magnificently in *McCulloch* v. *Maryland* (1819).

Even if he had tried, Marshall probably could not have kept politics out of the *Marbury* decision. He was faced by a severe political quandary, and any solution would probably have had to be political itself. John A. Garraty has speculated that Marshall may even have organized the appeal of the uncommissioned justices. If so, Marshall must either have been totally unaware of political realities in 1801, or else he was so finely honed politically that he had immediately conceived of the escape hatch which would convert apparent quandary into Federalist victory and had kept it secret for nearly two years. Neither seems likely. If we rule out these two extremes, Marshall would have been less likely than Jefferson to encourage the appeal for mandamus.

Until February 24, 1803, it seemed that Jefferson and the Republican party had more to gain from this case than John Marshall and the Federalists. Either the case would bring direct conflict between the executive and the judiciary at a time when Thomas Jefferson held all the high cards, or the judiciary would be forced to dismiss the case and thus validate the removal policies of Jefferson. To decide the case against Jefferson and Madison would expose the inability of the Supreme Court to enforce its mandate against an executive who ignored it. Judicial prestige would thus be shattered. To decide the case against Marbury would demonstrate that judicial power was a mirage from which no preservation of Federalist principles could be expected. Marshall's solution was to give Jefferson the decision he wanted and the tongue-lashing the Federalists wanted for him, and to give the Supreme Court the precedent for judicial review which Marshall so desperately wanted.

Thus it was political necessity, not the necessity of the case, which dictated the use of judicial review in *Marbury* v. *Madi-*

son. The certainty that the solidly Federalist Supreme Court must soon end necessitated fast action. Although the Marshall Court was not particularly old, the health of its members was not the best, and Marshall knew that when Federalists dropped off the Court they would be replaced with the same partisan care that he and John Adams had used earlier in packing the judiciary. Less than a year after the *Marbury* decision, Alfred Moore resigned because of ill health, and William Johnson of South Carolina started the parade of Republicans into the Supreme Court. As it turned out, Johnson was often a valued nationalist ally of Marshall, which came as a surprise to both Jefferson and Marshall. Other Republican justices also exasperated Jefferson by the frequency with which they sided with Marshall, though they would, nevertheless, be more hesitant than Marshall's Federalist phalanx of 1803 to affront a Republican Congress by voiding legislation.

MARSHALL'S THREE QUESTIONS

Marshall was able to do all that he did in the *Marbury* case because of his unorthodox approach to it. Marshall was an ardent advocate of the rhetorical question, but he did not care for those posed by Marbury's counsel, Charles Lee, because they all centered around the embarrassing question of jurisdiction. Lee's brief answered these three major questions:

"1st. Whether the Supreme Court can award the writ of mandamus in any case whatever?

"2nd. Whether it will lie to a Secretary of State in any case whatever?

"3rd. Whether, in the present case, the court may award a mandamus to James Madison, secretary of state?"

If Marshall had approached the case in this same manner, he could very quickly have made his case for judicial review by ruling that the Supreme Court had no jurisdiction in the case. This would have been no comfort to the aggrieved Marbury and, more important, to Marshall's Federalist friends who yearned to have Jefferson denounced for interfering with Federalist holders of federal offices.

Marshall announced instead that there would be "some departure in form, though not in substance" from the points so ably presented by Lee. He proposed to consider the case in this order:

"1st. Has the applicant a right to the commission he demands?" Marshall's forty-eight-paragraph answer was summed up in this concluding sentence: "1st. That by signing the commission of Mr. Marbury, the President of the United States appointed him a justice of peace for the county of Washington, in the District of Columbia; and that the seal of the United States, affixed thereto by the Secretary of State, is conclusive testimony of the verity of the appointment, and that the appointment conferred on him a legal right to the office for the space of five years."

"2d. If he has a right, and that right has been violated, do the laws of his country afford him a remedy?" Marshall answered this one in twenty-eight paragraphs, which are summed up in this concluding sentence: "2nd. That, having this legal title to the office, he has a consequent right to the commission; a refusal to deliver which is a plain violation of that right, for which the laws of his country afford him a remedy."

"3d. If they do afford him a remedy, is it a mandamus issuing from this court?" Marshall devoted thirty-two paragraphs to a demonstration that Marbury was entitled to a writ of mandamus and another forty-six paragraphs to an explanation of why he could not have it. This explanation, the most notable portion of the *Marbury* decision, will be the subject of most of the remainder of this chapter.

This approach to the case gave Marshall the interesting option of speaking out on all of the issues that he would eventually rule as outside the jurisdiction of the Supreme Court. He had made his point irregardless of nonjurisdiction. Marshall knew that he would be open to attack no matter how he approached the case. If he had ruled that the legislation grant-ing the Supreme Court the power to issue a writ of mandamus in such a case was unconstitutional without first considering whether Marbury had a legal right to it, he would have been accused of needlessly voiding an act of Congress. (An extreme reluctance to rule on the constitutionality of a legislative act if other grounds for a decision can be found is a fundamental principle of judicial review, one that even John Marshall professed. Sixteen years later, he assured his listeners that "in no doubtful case" would the Supreme Court rule legislation unconstitutional. Later he declared that when other grounds for a decision could be found, a court should avoid invalida-tion of legislation. He admitted in a private letter to Story in 1823 that he had avoided considering a law's constitutionality in circuit court because "it was not absolutely necessary" and, besides, "I am not fond of butting against a wall in sport.") The Jeffersonians would contend that Marshall had slyly evaded the issue of Marbury's legal right because he had none, and therefore the case was moot, and the exercise of judicial review was no precedent at all. Thomas Jefferson himself refuted every aspect of the decision, denying that Marbury had a right to the commission, that the Supreme Court could force its will on the executive branch by a writ of mandamus, and that the Supreme Court could control the legislature by "judi-cial veto." Thus Marshall would be damned if he did and damned if he didn't. Early in 1800 Marshall had remarked that whatever he did in the House of Representatives "the demo-crats will abuse me & therefore I need only to satisfy myself." There is no way of knowing if the same thought crossed his mind again in 1803, but he must have been very satisfied indeed with his decision in *Marbury* v. *Madison*.

PHILOSOPHY OF JUDICIAL REVIEW

Robert K. Faulkner wisely cautions against treating judicial review in *Marbury* v. *Madison* as entirely a memento of the political wars. Marshall played politics with great gusto in this opinion, but he was a warm advocate of judicial review long before Jefferson's election made it a political necessity. In the Virginia convention that ratified the United States Constitution in June 1788, he declared that only the judiciary could protect citizens from unconstitutional legislation. If Congress should "make a law not warranted by any of the powers enumerated, it would be considered by the judges as an infringement of the Constitution which they are to guard. They would not consider such a law as coming under their jurisdiction. They would declare it void." And that is precisely what the Marshall Court did fourteen years later to Section 13 of the Judiciary Act of 1789.*

Marshall's philosophy of judicial review is summarized in the final paragraphs of *Marbury* v. *Madison*. He began by attempting to undercut the inevitable argument that judicial review is an undemocratic meddling with the popular will; he insisted that the Constitution is the preeminent statement of the will of the American people. When they established a permanent framework of government the people knowingly set limits which were not to be exceeded. Therefore it is "a fundamental principle of our society" that legislation in conflict with the Constitution is void. Otherwise, written constitutions would be "absurd attempts, on the part of the people, to limit a power in its own nature illimitable."

As the judiciary functions to "say what the law is," it must judge between conflicting laws, including the highest law, the Constitution. Obviously the fundamental law must always prevail in such a contest. To rule otherwise would "subvert the

---

* The only time Marshall argued before the Supreme Court, in Ware v. Hylton, 3 Dallas 199 (1796), he asserted that "the judicial authority can have no right to question the validity of a law; unless such a jurisdiction is expressly given by the constitution." Then, however, he was speaking for his client rather than himself. Indeed, he was speaking against himself. If he had triumphed in *Ware* v. *Hylton*, he would have destroyed his own opportunity to profit from his purchase of the immense Fairfax estate.

very foundation of all written constitutions" and thus destroy "the greatest improvement on political institutions, a written constitution." Marshall then offers the *reductio ad absurdum,* hypothetical examples of blatant violations of the Constitution which would so obviously require judicial intervention that no one could question the Supreme Court's duty. If, for example, Congress were to levy an export tax, pass a bill of attainder or ex post facto law, or change the rules of evidence for treason (all of which are actions clearly banned by the Constitution), the Court must refuse to enforce such laws. Marshall did not call attention to the fact that the "unconstitutionality" of Section 13 of the Judiciary Act was not so clear-cut. Instead, the straw man with whom Marshall chose to debate was one who would deny judicial review under any circumstances. A more formidable hypothetical foe would have been a moderate who would agree that the Supreme Court must exercise review when there is a clear violation of the Constitution but who questioned whether Section 13 was a clear violation. As Robert McCloskey puts it, one of the intriguing political aspects of the *Marbury* decision is that it is "somewhat beside the point." It debated issues where there was little to debate and avoided the more prickly questions surrounding judicial review.

The oath taken by Supreme Court justices was offered as final evidence of their responsibility to void legislation in conflict with the Constitution they were sworn to uphold. Marshall did not explain why Presidents and congressmen, who took similar oaths, were required to support the Constitution as the judges understood it, rather than as their own consciences dictated. Nor did he point out that the extreme precautions he was taking against the threat of legislative supremacy might lead to judicial supremacy in the vitally important area of constitutional interpretation. Benjamin Hoadly, Bishop of Bangor, had warned in 1717 that "whoever hath an absolute *Authority* to *interpret* any written or spoken laws, it is he who is truly the Law-Giver to all intents and purposes, and not the

person who first wrote or spoke them." This statement is
almost inevitably the starting point for critics who regard judicial review as an undemocratic intrusion on the American system of government. If Marshall was acquainted with the
Hoadly axiom, he chose not to respond.

Marshall proved to his own satisfaction that it was "essential
to all written constitutions, that a law repugnant to the constitution is void" and that it was the function of the judiciary to
determine which laws were repugnant and which were not.
Believers in judicial review have, ever since, been persuaded
by his arguments. The easily persuaded Chancellor James Kent
thought it was "an argument approaching to the precision and
certainty of a mathematical demonstration." Nonbelievers
have complained, on the other hand, that "every argument
used by him in favor of judicial review begins by assuming the
whole ground in dispute." The nonbeliever's answer to Marshall's doctrine is ably summed up by J. A. C. Grant:

> Thus we are led to conclude, first, that the Court erred in pass-
> ing upon the legality of Marbury's claim to office before passing
> to the statute purporting to give it jurisdiction to hear the case;
> second, that the statute, properly construed, did not give the Court
> jurisdiction, and therefore raised no issue of constitutionality; and
> third, granting that the issue of constitutionality was involved, it
> was incorrectly decided.*

But even after blasting the soundness of *Marbury* v. *Madison,*
Grant must admit resentfully that its influence remains.

This decision has become a major foundation for judicial
review, one of the few distinctly American political ideas. Max
Lerner remarks, for instance, that "Marshall found judicial
review a moot question: he left it an integral part of the constitutional fabric." Because it has assumed such significance, it
is regrettable that Marshall broached the subject so light-
heartedly. He might better have cut back on his extensive

---

* "Marbury v. Madison Today," *American Political Science Review,*
XXIII (1929), 677–678.

discussion of mandamus and of the relationship between commissions and appointments to reserve time and energy for a more complete exposition of judicial review. An almost cavalier attitude pervades the paragraph that introduced this section:

> The question, whether an act, repugnant to the constitution, can become the law of the land, is a question deeply interesting to the United States; but, happily, not of an intricacy proportioned to its interest. It seems only necessary to recognize certain principles, supposed to have been long and well established, to decide it.*

He blithely assumed as "essential to all written constitutions" a judicial control of legislation which had existed nowhere but in America. Yet even today most countries with written constitutions have somehow managed to struggle along without American-style judicial review. Probably the political climate helped make Marshall so eager to treat judicial review as an accomplished fact rather than a debatable issue.

Perhaps John Marshall's great contribution to American political development is that he taught Americans to regard the Constitution as the starting point for all political action. In *Marbury* v. *Madison* he stressed the limitations established by the Constitution; later he would use the "uncertain and vague" language of the document to show Congress the opportunities for experimentation allowed by the Constitution. In either case, the Supreme Court would decide if and when the political branches exceeded their constitutional bounds. It would also be the sole judge of its own conduct.

THEORY OF REVIEW—NOT ITS HISTORY

Because of his lifelong worship of the Constitution, it is ironic that Marshall relied so little on constitutional clauses to support his view of judicial review. He mentions that the

---

* Marbury v. Madison, 1 Cranch 176 (1803).

power of the federal judiciary extends to all cases arising under
the Constitution; he cites a few examples of laws which would
be in clear violation of specific clauses of the Constitution; and
he speaks of the judges' oath to support the Constitution. But
if the framers of the Constitution had intended this to spell
out judicial review, their orthography was even worse than
usual for the eighteenth century. Marshall barely hints at the
supreme law clause ("This Constitution, and the Laws of
the United States which shall be made in Pursuance thereof;
and all Treaties made, or which shall be made, under the
Authority of the United States, shall be the supreme Law of
the land. . . ."), though it is the principal documentary justification which most historians have cited for judicial review.
He finds it more convenient to justify his doctrine by speaking
generically of constitutions rather than *the* Constitution.
Rather than *establishing* judicial review, the Constitution only
"confirms and strengthens the principle" which is basic to all
limited governments.

Marshall is equally imprecise in presenting the views of the
framers of the Constitution. They were in complete agreement
with Marshall regarding judicial review—at least that is the
implication in *Marbury* v. *Madison.* Marshall speaks only generally, however, about the views of those who wrote the Constitution, without ever naming names or quoting quotes. He
merely assumes, and invites his listeners to assume, that men
capable of framing such a Constitution *must* have intended for
the judiciary to enforce it by voiding unconstitutional legislation if necessary. Marshall seems to have been largely influenced by Alexander Hamilton's *Federalist No. 78,* though he
makes no acknowledgment even to this Founding Father.

Marshall likewise ignored judicial precedent. A number of
precedents of varying legitimacy could have been cited. State
courts had approached judicial review even before the framing
of the United States Constitution, and since then there had
been judicial review of sorts in a number of state courts
(Republican as well as Federalist) and in the lower federal

courts. The Supreme Court itself had hinted broadly at such authority by ruling a law constitutional, implying that it *might* have found it unconstitutional. Marshall had been in Philadelphia to observe Alexander Hamilton's advocacy of judicial review in that case, Hylton v. United States, 3 Dallas 171 (1796).

The associate justices who participated in the *Marbury* ruling had also been participants in some of these earlier cases, too. The *Philadelphia Aurora* speculated, probably erroneously, that it was William Paterson's voiding of legislation in Van Horne's Lessee v. Dorrance, 2 Dallas 304 (1795), in circuit court in Pennsylvania which had prevented his appointment as chief justice in 1801. William Cushing participated with Chief Justice John Jay in a 1792 circuit decision voiding Rhode Island legislation which violated the contract clause of the Constitution. In the Callender sedition trial in 1800, Samuel Chase anticipated many of the *Marbury* arguments for judicial review. Marshall had been present during that trial. Alfred Moore saw judicial review from the other side of the bench in North Carolina, for he was prosecuting attorney in Bayard v. Singleton, 1 Martin (N.C.) 5 (1787), one of the best known early precedents for judicial review. And of course Paterson, Cushing, and Chase all participated in *Hylton* v. *United States,* the case in which the Supreme Court reviewed a federal law and found it constitutional.

Once Marshall's judicial philosophy coincided with political advantage, there was sure to be an exercise of judicial review. The only question was what legislation would be voided. Marshall's contemporaries were probably not surprised by his show of judicial authority, though they must have been dumbfounded by the legislation he chose to invalidate. It was the latter part of Section 13 of the Federalist Judiciary Act of 1789:

> The Supreme Court . . . shall have power to issue writs of prohibition to the district courts, when proceeding as courts of admiralty and maritime jurisdiction, and writs of *mandamus,* in cases warranted by the principles and usages of law, to any courts appointed, or persons holding office under the authority of the United States.

Marshall ruled that Congress could not grant this power because the Constitution permits the Supreme Court to exercise original jurisdiction only in "cases affecting ambassadors, other public ministers and consuls, and those in which a state shall be a party." Otherwise, the Supreme Court is basically an appellate court. Until then no one had dreamed that there was anything faulty about Section 13. Even Marshall's adoring biographer, Albert J. Beveridge, thought it "a pretext which . . . had been unheard of and unsuspected hitherto." He conceded that "Nothing but the emergency compelling the insistence, at this particular time, that the Supreme Court has such a power, can fully and satisfactorily explain the action of Marshall in holding this section void." If Beveridge was surprised, then how must Thomas Jefferson have felt?

Marshall had a very good reason for avoiding precedents and other historical evidence this time, namely, because all of them were against him. The principal author of this "unconstitutional" legislation was Oliver Ellsworth, who was an important contributor to the writing of the Constitution and who preceded Marshall as chief justice. He should have been at least as authoritative as Marshall regarding the meaning of the Constitution. William Paterson was an active member of Ellsworth's judiciary committee during the writing of the Judiciary Act. Besides sitting at Marshall's side during the *Marbury* decision, Justice Paterson, like Ellsworth, had been a major contributor at the Federal Convention of 1787. Eleven other members of that same convention, including Marbury's nemesis James Madison and Marshall's mentor George Wythe, had supported the Judiciary Act in Congress. When Chief Justice John Jay protested certain unconstitutional aspects of the Judiciary Act of 1789—and note that he merely protested rather than voiding them—he took no notice of Section 13.

In his brief for the *Marbury* case, Charles Lee noted several instances where the Supreme Court had acted under Section 13 in the intervening years. The Court had not actually granted mandamus in these cases, but in refusing the judges gave no indication that mandamus would be unconstitutional. And a writ of prohibition under Section 13 had been granted. Three former members of the convention that framed the Constitution were on the Supreme Court when these Section 13 cases were heard, and in no instance were their ears offended by the unconstitutionality of the cases. Marshall could not have been unaware of these precedents, for in March 1802 Federalist Senator Samuel Dana cited them while expounding on Marbury's plight. Dana was stating sound pre-Marbury Federalist doctrine when he declared that "There does not appear to have been any question respecting the general power of the Supreme Court, to issue a mandamus to the Secretary of War, or any other subordinate official."

Marshall himself had participated earlier in an expansion of the Supreme Court's limited original jurisdiction which would seem from the *Marbury* opinion to be unconstitutional. The abortive judiciary bill that Marshall helped write in 1800 would have granted the Supreme Court jurisdiction over suits brought by "any state, body politic or corporate, company or person against the United States."

There was no need—other than political—to void Section 13. Marshall ruled that Congress had unconstitutionally expanded the original jurisdiction of the Supreme Court, so Marbury had come to the wrong court for a writ of mandamus. Marshall could have ruled instead that the authority to grant writs of mandamus applied only in appellate cases or in those few instances where the Supreme Court already had original jurisdiction.* The decision regarding Marbury's commission would

---

* This was the view taken by the Supreme Court in similar cases involving Section 14 of the Judiciary Act in 1813 and 1821. Justice William Johnson wrote both opinions, but Marshall apparently concurred. Both the Judiciary Act of 1801, which Marshall helped to write, and the Judicial Code of 1911 used wording similar to the disputed Section 13, though they concluded by specifically limiting the power of mandamus to cases in which the Supreme Court had jurisdiction.

still have been the same, but Marshall would have lost the opportunity to void a federal law.

Furthermore, Marshall did not quote all of the pertinent clause of the Constitution. To be sure, the limited list of areas of original jurisdiction for the Supreme Court is followed in Article III, Section 2, by the statement that "in all the other Cases before mentioned, the supreme Court shall have appellate Jurisdiction." This, however, is followed by a qualification which Marshall ignores: ". . . with such Exceptions, and under such Regulations as the Congress shall make." The writ of mandamus in Section 13 could have been ruled to be one of those exceptions. Here, at least, Marshall was consistent with his earlier views. He felt in 1803 as he had in 1788 that the only "exceptions . . . Congress shall make" were to decrease appellate jurisdiction rather than to increase original jurisdiction. But the clause could as well have meant the latter. Marshall himself ruled eighteen years later in *Cohens* v. *Virginia* that to give the "distributive clause" as strict an interpretation as he himself had given it in 1803 "would, in some instances, defeat the obvious intention of the article." He argued unconvincingly that his 1821 ruling was not really inconsistent with "some *dicta* of the court, in the case of *Marbury* v. *Madison*."

Perhaps the most startling aspect of Marshall's *Marbury* coup was that while he appeared daring in his assertion of judicial power, his action was, nevertheless, remarkably safe. He had chosen the grounds for his showdown with Jefferson so shrewdly that there was nothing the Republican President and Congress would, or probably could, do about it. Robert McCloskey aptly describes the decision as "a masterwork of indirection, a brilliant example of Marshall's capacity to sidestep danger while seeming to court it, to advance in one direction while his opponents are looking in another." The Republicans had expected Marshall to *try* to save Marbury's job. Instead, Marshall sweetened his criticism of Jefferson and his assertion of judicial review by deciding the case against

Marbury. Jefferson, already terribly worried about Napoleon's acquisition of New Orleans, could not get too worked up about a case which he had technically won. Best of all, the decision required no implementation. If the Supreme Court had ruled that Congress had unconstitutionally repealed the Judiciary Act of 1801 it would be challenged somehow to restore the act and put the Midnight judges back on their restored benches. This would have been impossible and the weakness of the Supreme Court would have become public knowledge. But to implement the *Marbury* decision, all that was required was to see that Marbury did not regain his commission and position. In the current political setting, this was an easy matter.

Furthermore, this instance of judicial review did not even violate Jefferson's own concept of constitutional decision-making. Jefferson believed that each department of government—executive, legislature, and judiciary—should determine constitutionality within its own sphere. The Supreme Court was clearly acting within the judicial sphere when it refused to carry out a section of the Judiciary Act of 1789. Besides, the Supreme Court *appeared* to be shunning authority rather than seizing it. It was brilliantly reassuring strategy to initiate the voiding of federal legislation by piously refusing to accept power which Congress had wrongfully attempted to give the Court. Better yet, the legislation to be voided had been enacted by the Federalists rather than the Republicans.

More than a half-century passed before the Supreme Court again ruled federal legislation unconstitutional. Throughout that period the Court never expanded on Marshall's doctrine, but merely took it for granted. By the time that the Supreme Court finally came to exercise the power which Marshall had asserted, it was generally taken for granted in the legal profession (and this includes Congress) that it possessed the power of judicial review. For all its political tricks and legal errors, then, *Marbury* v. *Madison* is a great historic event. One of its major critics, Alexander Bickel, concludes that "It is hallowed.

It is revered. If it had a physical presence, like the Alamo or Gettysburg, it would be a tourist attraction." Chief Justice Earl Warren believed that "Perhaps the greatest contribution [Marshall] made to our system of jurisprudence was the establishment of an independent judiciary through the principle of judicial review. In a case instituted the first year of his incumbency, he rooted this fundamental principle in American constitutional law as our original contribution to the science of law." Clearly an immense growth has come from a very tiny seed—the mysterious commission of William Marbury. But in 1803 it remained to be seen whether Thomas Jefferson could uproot the seed before it was too late.

9

JEFFERSONIANS REVIEW
THE JUDICIARY

———————◆•◆———————

John Marshall conducted his duel with President Jefferson so shrewdly that when the *Marbury* decision was completed remarkably few onlookers seemed to know just what had happened. At first the Republicans did not know where, or whether, to hit back. And Federalists who might have wanted to praise their judicial warriors did not know just what portions of the decision to praise—except, of course, the criticism of Jefferson. Contemporary newspapers demonstrated a confusion which was probably typical of the country as a whole. All that was clear was that the six Federalists still clung to their bench, even after lecturing the supposedly omnipotent Jefferson and his Congress. The next step was left to Jefferson.

CONTEMPORARY REACTIONS TO
MARBURY V. *MADISON*

Historians of the Marshall Court have long debated the contemporary response to *Marbury* v. *Madison*. Albert J.

Beveridge was dumbfounded by the apparent disinterest in it. He complained that Marshall's first great decision "received scant notice at the time of its delivery. The newspapers had little to say about it. Even the bench and the bar of the country, at least in the sections remote from Washington, appear not to have heard of it, or, if they had, to have forgotten it." Charles Warren, on the other hand, felt that the decision received extensive newspaper coverage. Later historians have borrowed the attitude and evidence of either one or the other. Actually, there is truth in both positions. The *Marbury* decision was printed at immense length in a number of newspapers, both Federalist and Republican. However, these accounts are extremely frustrating for the historian seeking more than mere repetition of the decision. Generally, they provide neither the insightful contemporary comment which is bread and butter to the historian, nor the foolish misconception which is his dessert. They merely plod through the decision without even the pretense of editorial comment. It has been speculated that the case was slighted because of the editors' preoccupation with worsening diplomatic relations with France. But if New Orleans bumped *Marbury* v. *Madison* out of the newspapers, it is difficult to explain how editors found space for page after page of the decision. More likely, the editors simply did not know what to write about the case, so they fulfilled their obligation to inform the public by merely reprinting "this interesting and highly important opinion," leaving it for the reader to decide what was interesting or important about it.

The newspapers of the District of Columbia, whose readers were most concerned with the fate of the uncommissioned justices of the peace, provide an accurate index of newspaper response to the case. As might be expected, the most extensive coverage was given by the *National Intelligencer,* Jefferson's pet journal, and by the *Washington Federalist,* which was Marshall's favorite.

On December 21, 1801, the *Intelligencer* reported on the first mandamus hearing, without comment and without even mentioning the local individuals involved. Like nearly every other journal in the country, it gave extensive coverage in 1802 to the debates in Congress regarding the repeal of the Judiciary Act; sometimes these debates verged on the mandamus issue. The petition of Marbury, Ramsay, and Hooe in January 1803, requesting evidence to be used in their judicial case, likewise received extensive nationwide attention. The week before the *Marbury* case was to be argued before the Supreme Court, the *Intelligencer* attributed the case to Federalist vengeance and greed. It added that Adams "declined" issuing their commissions "for what reasons is not understood," implying that more than mere carelessness was involved. Thus Jefferson's only choice seemed to be to make new appointments or implement an action by Adams which, "if it did not violate the letter, certainly did violate the spirit and the end of the Constitution." Naturally, no righteous President could choose the latter. On February 14 the one-sided arguments in the *Marbury* case were reported without comment. On February 28, four days after the decision, the *Intelligencer* did the same as nearly every other newspaper in the country. It listed Marshall's three questions and briefly summarized his answers. Regarding the key question involving judicial review it stated only that "on the third question, it was determined, that the act of Congress giving the power to the Supreme Court, to issue a writ of mandamus in such a case, was unconstitutional, and consequently void." From March 18 to 25 it devoted more than eighteen columns (nearly four complete pages) to the publication of the entire decision. That was the end of its coverage, for it offered no editorial comment whatever on the decision. The *Intelligencer* did, however, reprint the "Littleton" essays, which are described below.

Although the *Washington Federalist* slighted the pretrial aspects of the case, the newspaper gave the final decision its most laudatory account. The day after Marshall's decision, the *Federalist* stated it was impressed by the decision's "great ability" and apparently twice as impressed (because the paper reiterated this point) by its "great length." Two weeks later came the promised editorial comment:

> . . . it will remain as a monument of the wisdom, impartiality and independence of the Supreme Court. . . . The important principles resulting from the particular structure of our government, which are there examined and settled—the ability with which these principles are investigated—the strength and reason with which they are supported, and the perspicuous, yet nervous stile in which they are delivered, must excite in every American, an honest pride, at seeing their courts of Judicature, those guardians of their property, lives and reputation, supplied with such talents, and animated with so laudable a zeal for the rights and liberties of the citizen.*

Obviously, the *Federalist* was impressed, but it was not yet clear by exactly what—other than length. If it was the exercise of judicial review which excited the editor, he was not yet ready to let everyone else in on the secret. Ironically, the *Federalist* also published one of the few systematic attacks on Marshall's theory of judicial review, but this letter was prefaced with the editorial assumption that the legitimacy of review was "almost too clear for controversy; and when elucidated by the able opinion of the Supreme Court, scepticism itself could no longer doubt." This journal published the entire decision in its issues of March 17 to March 22.

The poorest coverage of the case was given by the *Alexandria Gazette*. It might have been expected to be most concerned because three of the original four plaintiffs were, like the *Gazette* itself, Alexandria Federalists. It made occasional passing references to the pretrial issues, but without ever providing the obvious local news peg. The day after the opinion was rendered, the *Gazette* reached the strange conclusion that "the judges of the Supreme Court have given it as their

---

* *Washington Federalist,* March 11, 1803.

opinion, in the case of the Mandamus, that the justices are entitled to their commissions, but, that they have not the power to issue a mandamus in the District of Columbia, it not being a State; if, however, the occurrence had taken place in one of the states they should have had no hesitation in granting it." After this sorry attempt at interpretive reporting, perhaps it is fortunate that the *Gazette* merely printed the decision in March rather than explaining it.

Although several Federalist newspapers crowed over Marshall's gratuitous lecture to the President, they showed no excitement over the voiding of a Federalist law. On March 5, 1803, the *Charleston Daily Courier* began a long and heated editorial on the "factious injustice" of the Senate's rejection of Marbury's petition for information regarding the commissions; it was continued through the issues of March 6, 7, and 8. On March 11 the *Courier* announced the result of the "interesting and highly important" *Marbury* opinion, promising to add more later. But the only addition was the publication of the entire opinion in the issues of March 30 to April 1. More typical were the *Maryland Gazette,* which offered a brief summary without comment, and the *Providence Gazette* and *Connecticut Courant,* which simply ignored it. If there is truth in the story that the Republicans were outraged by the exercise of judicial review and the Federalists overjoyed, the party scribes were not aware of it.

Other Federalists seemed equally oblivious to the "victory" won by Marshall. Mrs. William Cushing, who regularly wrote long letters about judicial activities to Mrs. John Adams, did not even refer to the case in the letters she wrote after the 1803 term. If there was Federalist applause, it had not reached the New York home of that old Federalist war-horse Gouverneur Morris. Months after *Marbury* v. *Madison,* Morris continued to believe that the repeal act had overthrown the judiciary and that the House of Representatives was absolute sovereign. Early in 1804 he still felt that the Constitution had received a

"mortal stab" through the "prostration of the judiciary" in
1802. The Constitution still suffered from that same "mortal
wound" at the end of 1804. Obviously Morris did not recognize *Marbury* v. *Madison* as a salve for these grievous wounds.

North Carolinians John Steele and Nathaniel Macon took
positions directly opposite to the accepted view of party
response to the *Marbury* decision. General Steele wrote Macon
to protest the "fashionable doctrine that the courts have
power to pronounce acts of Congress unconstitutional and
void," and Macon defended judicial review. As Steele was a
North Carolina Federalist who had recently been comptroller
of the United States Treasury, he might be expected to have
been delighted by the decision. Instead, he accused the
Supreme Court of attempting to subject the nation to the
discipline of a "department which, in theory, is the third,
but in practice aims at becoming the first power of the
State." Macon, who was Republican Speaker of the United
States House of Representatives, remained consistent with his
view in 1798 that the judiciary could and should void the
hateful Sedition Act. Macon gave the "non-Republican" response that the judges have authority to determine matters of
constitutionality, although every declaration of the unconstitutionality of a law is done "at their peril." He was, of course,
pleased by the outcome, though the decision reminded him of
"a noted member of Congress who always spoke on one side
and voted on the other."

Macon did not object to the voiding of federal legislation.
He was disturbed by the threat that if the Supreme Court had
jurisdiction it would attempt to control the executive through
mandamus. This attitude was typical among those few Republicans who bothered to record their response to *Marbury* v.
Madison. They were pleased that Jefferson had "won" the
case, shocked that the judiciary would dare to intrude upon
the executive in this manner, and nonchalant about judicial
review, if they recognized it at all. This, despite the fact that

only a year before, during the debates on repeal of the
Judiciary Act of 1801, Republicans had argued vehemently
that they would not tolerate judicial interference. If the
Supreme Court had voided the repeal act in *Stuart* v. *Laird,*
rather than a minor segment of the Judiciary Act of 1789 in
Marbury v. *Madison,* Republican congressmen would not have
been so blasé about Marshall's foot-in-the-doorway move to
judicial power. The political wisdom of Marshall's selection
of which law to void saved him and his Court. Even the
Marshall Court played down the *Marbury* precedent for judicial review. In the nine decisions in which *Marbury* v. *Madison*
was cited during Marshall's judicial career, it was always
used as a precedent for discussions of mandamus or jurisdiction. It was ignored—or taken for granted!—as a precedent
for judicial review.

One of the better Republican critiques of the case, by
Littleton in the *Virginia Argus,* regarded *Marbury* v. *Madison*
as grotesque. It urged Marshall to deny paternity of this
"hideous monster; its conception in giants size, its succeeding
years dwindling it into nothing; Its head in the rear; its tail
in front; its legs mounted on high to support the burthen,
while its back was destined to tread the earth, its bowels in
the exterior, and its hide in the interior." Marshall's discussion of the issues without jurisdiction, "contrary to all law,
precedent and principle," was especially grotesque to Littleton.
He agreed that the Court lacked jurisdiction and thus, by
implication, he approved judicial review. Littleton's critique
was reprinted in the leading Republican newspapers.

JEFFERSON'S RESPONSE TO
MARBURY V. *MADISON*

In a way it is regrettable that so many of Jefferson's closest
political associates had trooped off to Washington with him.
If James Madison, for instance, had been at home in Virginia

when the *Marbury* decision was rendered, Jefferson would unquestionably have written to Madison of his personal views on it. They were such splendid correspondents that it is a severe loss to American historiography when they were in the same city, exchanging ideas face to face rather than by mail. Because of the lack of evidence we can only surmise that Jefferson, like other Republicans, was most upset by judicial interference with the executive. Jefferson's relations with Republican congressmen and newspapers were so intimate that if he had strong feelings about the exercise of judicial review they would soon have found expression in Congress or the *National Intelligencer.*

A year and a half after *Marbury* v. *Madison,* Jefferson briefly discussed judicial review in a letter to Mrs. John Adams, but without any mention of Marshall's recent decision. Regarding judicial review of the Sedition Act, he declared that "nothing in the constitution has given them a right to decide for the executive, more than to the Executive to decide for them. both magistracies are equally independant in the sphere of action assigned to them." Clearly, Jefferson adhered to his doctrine of departmental interpretation of the Constitution. He reiterated the point in the same letter: "But the opinion which gives to the judges the right to decide what laws are constitutional, and what not, not only for themselves in their own sphere of action, but for the legislature & executive also, in their spheres, would make the judiciary a despotic branch." As he did not bring up the *Marbury* case, it is evident that, at least in 1804, the judicial review exercised in *Marbury* v. *Madison* was acceptable to Jefferson because the Supreme Court was interpreting legislation involving its own judicial sphere.* This attitude probably accounts for the Republicans' lack of concern about the "limited" review in

---

* Jefferson to Abigail Adams, September 11, 1804, Massachusetts Historical Society: Adams Papers.

Marbury v. *Madison*. Furthermore, Marshall's decision was so politic that even if they were upset there was little they could have done but grumble.

The treason trial of Aaron Burr in 1807, over which Chief Justice Marshall presided in circuit court at Richmond, Virginia, ended Jefferson's silent acquiescence in the *Marbury* decision. When Jefferson learned that the *Marbury* decision was being cited as precedent, he hustled off a letter to District Attorney George Hay demanding that citation of this case as authority be stopped "at the threshold." He had "long wished for a proper occasion to have the gratuitous opinion in Marbury *v.* Madison brought before the public & denounced as not law." This task he now assigned to Hay. Jefferson insisted that the decision was extrajudicial because "the judges in the outset [a misstatement] disclaimed all cognisance of the case; altho' they then went on to say what would have been their opinion, had they had cognisance of it." Even if the Supreme Court had had jurisdiction, it would have been unlawful to issue a mandamus for the commissions because "to a commission, a deed, a bond, *delivery* is essential to give validity." While a commission is still in the hands of the executive he can cancel it for any reason—or no reason. Finally, "the Constitution intended that the three great branches of the government should be co-ordinate, & independant of each other. as to acts therefore which are to be done by either, it has given no controul to another branch."*At that same time, when Attorney General Caesar Augustus Rodney cited *Marbury* v. *Madison* as a precedent in a letter to Jefferson, the President did not even answer him.

Marshall offended Virginians countless times in the ensuing decades, but most of all in 1821, when he asserted jurisdiction in *Cohens* v. *Virginia,* a lottery case which Virginia Judge Spencer Roane insisted could not be appealed to federal

---

* Jefferson to Hay, June 2, 1807, Library of Congress: Jefferson Papers.

courts. This decision engendered angry pamphlets attacking Marshall personally, as well as his decision. No response was hotter than the private correspondence of Thomas Jefferson. Even before the *Cohens* decision, Jefferson had warned that to regard the judges as "the ultimate arbiters of all constitutional questions" is "a very dangerous doctrine indeed, and one which would place us under the despotism of an Oligarchy." He harkened back to *Marbury* v. *Madison* when he noted that the judges had "at times over-stepped their limit by undertaking to command executive officers in the discharge of their executive duties." One of the things which he insisted the Supreme Court could not force the President to do is "to issue requisite commissions." He may also have been thinking of the author of that decision when he added that Supreme Court justices "have, with others, the same passions for party, for power, and the privileges of their corps."

After the *Cohens* decision Jefferson wrote lengthy epistles to Justice William Johnson, the first Supreme Court justice whom he had appointed, attempting to persuade him to lead the Court back to the gospel of Republicanism as interpreted by Jefferson. He also urged James Madison to apply similar pressure upon his friends on the Court. On June 12, 1823, Jefferson turned briefly from the *Cohens* decision to give Johnson his view of *Marbury* v. *Madison,* a decision rendered a year before Johnson came on the Court. This is Jefferson's most extended commentary on the case:

> This practice of Judge Marshall of travelling out of his case to prescribe what the law would be in a moot case not before the court, is very irregular and very censurable. I recollect another instance, and the more particularly perhaps, because it in some measure bore on myself. among the midnight appointments of mr Adams, were commissions to some federal justices of the peace for Alexandria. these were signed and sealed by him, but not delivered. I found them on the table of the department of State, on my entrance into office, and I forbade their delivery. Marbury, named in one of them, applied to the Supreme court for a Mandamus to

the Secretary of State, (mr. Madison) to deliver the commission intended for him. the court determined at once that being an original process, they had no cognisance of it; and there the question before them was ended. but the Chief Justice went on to lay down what the law would be, had they jurisdiction of the case, to wit, that they should command the delivery. the object was clearly to instruct any other court having the jurisdiction, what they should do, if Marbury should apply to them. besides the impropriety of this gratuitous interference, could any thing exceed the perversion of law? for if there is any principle of law never yet contradicted, it is that delivery is one of the essentials to the validity of a deed. altho signed and sealed, yet as long as it remains in the hands of the party himself, it is *in fieri* only, it is not a deed, and can be made so only by his [its] delivery. in the hands of a third person it may be made an escrow. but whatever is in the executive offices is certainly deemed to be in the hands of the President; and in this case, was actually in my hands, because, when I countermanded them, there was as yet no Secretary of state. yet this case of Marbury and Madison is continually cited by bench & bar, as if it were settled law, without any animadversion on its being merely an obiter dissertation of the Chief Justice.*

THE WEAPON OF IMPEACHMENT

To no one's surprise, impeachment was the initial Republican response to Federalist flexing of judicial muscles. The victorious Republicans had already found impeachment a useful device for dispensing with Federalist judges at the state level, especially in Pennsylvania. Shortly after the *Marbury* decision was announced, a Republican newspaper in Boston warned that the judges must be impeached if they dared to issue a writ of mandamus to the secretary of state; clearly, this warning was written before the *Marbury* decision, even though it was not printed until two weeks afterward. Mandamus was said to be "no less than a commencement of war between the constituted departments." Either the Court

---

* Jefferson to Johnson, June 12, 1823, Library of Congress: Jefferson Papers.

must "retreat from the attack; or march on, till they incur an impeachment and removal from office." During the debates regarding repeal of the Judiciary Act of 1801, several Republicans in Congress had intimated that the justices would be impeached if they interfered. The Supreme Court neither interfered with the repeal act nor issued a command to the executive in *Marbury* v. *Madison,* so for the moment the justices were safe from impeachment. At the same time as the *Marbury* case, though, the Republican executive and Congress initiated an experiment with judicial impeachment which some believed would eventually expand to the Marshall Court.

Only a week before the Supreme Court heard the *Marbury* case, President Jefferson hinted broadly that Congress should impeach District Judge John Pickering of New Hampshire. In 1787 John Pickering was one of four New Hampshire delegates elected to the Convention which framed the United States Constitution. If he had attended the Convention at Philadelphia he would have been one of the Founding Fathers, rather than a mere inebriated and insane jurist, who would be the first United States official to be impeached and removed from office. In 1788 Pickering played a prominent role in the New Hampshire convention which ratified the Constitution and thus (being the ninth state to ratify) brought the United States under the Constitution of 1787 officially into being. Perhaps as a reward for this service, Pickering was appointed a United States district judge in 1795. Despite numerous eccentricities, he performed his duties adequately until 1800, when his conduct on the bench became literally insane. Jefferson forwarded some longstanding complaints against Pickering to "the House of Representatives, to whom the Constitution has confided a power of instituting proceedings of redress, if they shall be of opinion that the case calls for them." The House established a committee to study the charges the same day that it received Jefferson's suggestion. The committee report was presented on February 18, and the House impeached the wild judge by a vote of 48 to 8 on March 2, the day before adjournment and only six days after the *Marbury* decision. Because the House had acted "at so late a period of the session," the Senate's impeachment trial did not begin until January 4, 1804. It found Pickering "guilty as charged," without determining whether the "charge" constituted "high Crimes and Misdemeanors," and removed him from office. Thus the impeachment process gave Jefferson an early taste of victory over the Federalist judiciary.

Pickering probably did not deserve to be impeached; he had committed no "high Crimes and Misdemeanors," which are the constitutional bases for impeachment. Yet he certainly did not deserve to sit on any judicial bench. Whether his drunkenness was caused by insanity or his insanity by drunkenness, the combination made him totally unfit to be a judge. The principal defense offered by Jacob Pickering was that at the time of the offenses charged against his father, Judge Pickering "was, and for more than two years before, and ever since has been, and now is, insane, his mind wholly deranged, and altogether incapable of transacting any kind of business which requires the exercise of judgment, or the faculties of reason; and, therefore, that the said John Pickering is incapable of corruption of judgment, no subject of impeachment, or amenable to any tribunal for his actions." Later, the son added that the judge's derangement was "constant and permanent, every day of his life completely demonstrating his insanity." Besides being too insane to perform his duties on the bench, Judge Pickering was apparently also too far-gone to resign his office, as a timely resignation had never been suggested as a way to avoid dismissal.

Pickering's scandalous conduct was a familiar story to John Marshall. In January 1801, when Jeremiah Smith of New Hampshire wrote to ask Marshall to support his candidacy as one of the new circuit judges, he remarked that "the district Judge has been deranged in his mind for the year past & his malady has every appearance of continuing through life. We have had no district Court for a year." Smith urged that the then pending Judiciary Act should include a clause granting extra jurisdiction to the circuit judge "during Mr. Pickering's disability." The rescinded Judiciary Act of 1801 did briefly solve the Pickering problem. Section 25 provided that "in case of the inability of the district judge of either of the districts of the United States to perform the duties of his office," his duties would be performed by one of the circuit judges. Jeremiah Smith took Pickering's place during the year that the Act of 1801 was in effect. Its repeal returned Smith to the bar and Pickering to the bench. Indirectly, then, it was the Republicans who placed the mad Federalist on the bench, for Pickering seems only to have been a neurotic Federalist in 1795 when Washington appointed him.

THE IMPEACHMENT OF JUSTICE CHASE

After this initial success with the impeachment process, Jefferson turned to bigger game. Two months after Pickering's removal, Jefferson brought Justice Samuel Chase's "extraordinary charge . . . to the grand jury at Baltimore" to the attention of Joseph H. Nicholson, a Republican representative from Maryland. At Baltimore, Chase apparently railed against universal suffrage, which was converting the American republic into an "ignorant mobocracy," "the worst of all possible governments." According to the *National Intelligencer,* Chase also "went into an assertion of the right of the judiciary to decide on the constitutionality of laws," but this was the one section of Chase's remarks on which the newspaper chose not to editorialize. A Republican observer claims that Chase described the Jefferson administration as weak and inadequate and said its sole concern was retention of its "unfairly acquired power," though Chase later denied making such an attack on the administration. Jefferson thought "this seditious & official attack on the principles of our Constitution, and on the proceedings of a State" should be punished. To whom should the public look for redress besides a Maryland Republican in Congress—such as Nicholson? "I ask these questions for your consideration," he concluded. "For myself, it is better that I should not interfere."

Congress was adjourned at the time, so it was not until January 1804 that impeachment action was initiated by John Randolph of Virginia. The House voted to impeach Chase on March 12, 1804, and the trial in the Senate began on February 4, 1805. Besides Chase's charge to the Baltimore grand jury, most of the other grounds of impeachment concerned Chase's gross conduct in the *Fries* and *Callender* sedition trials (1800) at Philadelphia and Richmond, respectively. In a period of a few weeks Chase had so browbeaten defense counsel in these trials that they simply walked away from his circuit courtrooms. On March 1 the Senate failed on eight separate votes to convict Chase. Although twenty-three adverse votes were required to remove him, the largest total recorded against him was only nineteen; this vote concerned the charge regarding Chase's political harangue at Baltimore. On two other charges the majority voted eighteen to sixteen against him, far short of the required two-thirds majority. Several Republicans bucked party leadership because, while they did not condone Chase's conduct, neither did they see it as "high Crimes and Misdemeanors." Also, Chase was ably defended by a battery of skilled Federalist lawyers—two of them Midnight judges—whereas the prosecution was led by the erratic John Randolph.

Senator John Quincy Adams, who cast the first nay vote on each of the eight charges against Chase, sincerely believed that if the Republicans succeeded in removing one justice they would persist until all the Federalists were gone. It is impossible, however, to imagine as strong a case being made against Marshall, Washington, Paterson, or Cushing as could be made against Chase. John Marshall was as fully a political being as Samuel Chase, for instance, but they differed completely in style. Marshall's weapon was the stiletto. His technique was amply demonstrated in *Marbury* v. *Madison* where he thrust and withdrew his weapon before the enemy knew he had been pierced. Chase's political weapon, on the other hand, was the sledge hammer—roundhouse blows of coarse and blatantly partisan language. Although Marshall was as concerned as Chase about the irrevocable march of democracy in America, he was too wise to antagonize the American democracy with antidemocratic lectures.

John Quincy Adams did not make a practice of defending Thomas Jefferson. Years later, however, he expressed doubts that Jefferson was involved in the impeachment plot. Although Jefferson "did not discountenance the impeachment" of Chase, Adams concluded, "it was generally believed that he did not favour the conviction of the judge." Obviously, Jefferson was successful in carrying out his role as one who "should not interfere" in impeachments if even Adams could not find him out. This was one of those rare occasions when an Adams erred by thinking the better of someone, rather than the worse. Jefferson was outraged at the lack of party discipline which saved Chase's judicial life. He did not express his rage then; nor did he attempt to quell the outbursts of Republican newspapers such as the *Richmond Enquirer, Boston Independent Chronicle,* and *Philadelphia Aurora,* which railed against the Senate's failure to remove Chase.

Sometimes Chase was as embarrassing to his Federalist colleagues on the bench as he was antagonizing to the Republicans. On one occasion Chief Justice Oliver Ellsworth had to rebuke his flamboyant associate publicly before counsel could continue. District Judge Richard Peters, who was momentarily linked with Chase in the House's impeachment investigation

because they had sat together in the *Fries* trial, complained
that of all the justices "I like the least to be coupled with
[Chase]. I never sat with him without Pain, as he was forever
getting into some intemperate and unnecessary Squabble. If
I am to be immolated let it be with some other Victim—or
for my own Sins." In 1816 Peters recalled once giving Chase
"a complete Tongue lashing; after sharing in the Consequences of one of his hasty Measures which I highly &
decidedly disapproved."

While Pickering was being tried in the Senate, and the
House was getting ready to impeach Chase, Midnight Judge
Jeremiah Smith's principal concern was for Marshall and
Paterson. He felt the Jeffersonians hated them more than
Chase because Marshall and Paterson were more reputable.
He wanted to know from Senator William Plumer of New
Hampshire if the two justices were frightened. If Smith had
asked a year later, during the Chase trial, Plumer would
undoubtedly have replied that Marshall, at least, was terrified.
Plumer was greatly disappointed with Marshall's appearance
before the High Court of Impeachment on February 16, 1805:

> The Chief Justice really discovered too much caution—too much
> fear—too much cunning—He ought to have been more bold—
> frank & explicit than he was. There was in his manner an evident
> disposition to accomodate the Managers. That dignified frankness
> which his high office required did not appear. A cunning man
> ought never to discover the arts of the *trimmer* in his testimony.*

Marshall's testimony, as presented in the *Annals of Congress,*
does not appear to justify Plumer's attack. He answered re-
spectfully and directly, neither evading the questions nor
twisting them into a platform from which he could defend
Chase. He frequently admitted only a vague recollection of
the events about which he was testifying, but the passage of
five years since the Callender trial would account for this.

* Everett S. Brown, ed., *William Plumer's Memorandum of Proceedings
in the United States Senate, 1803–1807* (New York: Macmillan, 1923), p. 291.

Plumer possibly felt that it was the chief justice's duty to be an advocate for his brother justice rather than merely answer questions. Plumer was "much better pleased" with the testimony of William Marshall, a brother of the chief justice, because on five of the eight charges he gave "a complete defence of the accused." In contrast, John Marshall sometimes came close to criticizing Chase.

It may have been *how* Marshall testified, rather than *what* he said, that upset Plumer. John Randolph, House manager of the case against Chase implied that Marshall may have looked less sympathetic to Chase than he sounded: "What said the Chief Justice? And, if I may say so, *what did he look?* He felt all the delicacy of his situation, and as he could not approve, he declined giving any opinion on the demeanor of his associate." Marshall was very uneasy about the threat which the Chase impeachment presented to his Court. Excessively impolitic, yet grotesquely partisan, Justice Chase provided a large and slow-moving target for the enemies of the Supreme Court. Like Ellsworth and Peters, the chief justice realized that such conduct made Chase a very shaky pillar for the judicial edifice Marshall was building.

Marshall found the charges against Chase alarming to "the friends of a pure and of course an independent judiciary, if among those who rule our land there be any of that description." Less than three weeks before his own testimony, Marshall wrote a remarkable letter to Chase protesting "the present doctrine . . . that a Judge giving a legal opinion contrary to the opinion of the legislature is liable to impeachment." Marshall showed just how frightened he really was when he suggested that in such a case "the modern doctrine of impeachment should yield to an appellate jurisdiction in the legislature. A reversal of those legal opinions deemd unsound by the legislature would certainly better comport with the mildness of our character than a removal of the judge who has renderd them unknowing of his fault." Thus in a private letter, which Chase had the good sense to keep private, Marshall condoned legislative supremacy in constitutional interpretation. How interested Jefferson would have been in this statement! And what a strange addendum Marshall was writing to the theory of judicial review which he had so confidently expounded only two years earlier in *Marbury* v. *Madison*! Evidently he was not so confirmed in his advocacy of judicial review that he was prepared to risk the independence of his Federalist Court to fight for it; like Judge Peters, Marshall had no desire to go down with Chase. As this was Marshall's mood on January 23, it is not surprising if he appeared timid when he appeared before the Senate on February 16.

The fact that Representative John Randolph, Marshall's cousin, chose Marshall as the honorable judge to be contrasted with the dishonorable Chase probably rubbed salt in the wounds of Federalist senators who were fighting for Chase's survival. Marshall must have been as surprised as Jefferson and Plumer to hear himself described in the rambling discourse with which Randolph closed the argument as "the able and excellent judge, whose worth was never fully known until he was raised to the bench."

The chief justice himself was proposed by some as the next victim of impeachment. Early in 1807, when some of Aaron Burr's accomplices were freed by the Supreme Court, Representative Willis Alston of North Carolina threatened to impeach all the justices, but this threat was only loose talk. Later that year, during the Burr treason trial, District Attorney George Hay made several references to Samuel Chase's trial which might have been interpreted as a warning to Marshall. When Hay was called on this point by defense counsel, he denied that any threat had been intended. Marshall mildly replied that he had not regarded Hay's remarks as "any personal allusion." The administration press was more obvious in its thrust. When Burr was acquitted, William Thompson, writing under the name "Lucius," published a number of "Letters to John Marshall" which were reprinted in many Republican journals. Lucius demanded the removal of Marshall, though without specifying the method, because Marshall and Burr were "traitors in heart and in fact." A Republican toast of the day took up the cry: "The judiciary when they Marshall themselves on the side of treason, in opposition to law, justice and humanity. May they hear the 'small, still voice' of the nation ordering them from their unhallowed seats into eternal political oblivion."

"A FARCE WHICH WILL NOT BE TRIED AGAIN"

Because Jefferson did not leash his party editors, some historians assume that Jefferson was directing them. Actually, he appears to have lost confidence in impeachment as a means of disciplining the judiciary. During the Burr trial he wrote to William Branch Giles, a Virginia senator who had been a leading advocate of Chase's removal, that "impeachment is a farce which will not be tried again." He hoped instead that the judiciary's protection of Burr would force Congress to "amend the error in our constitution which makes any branch independant of the nation."

Jefferson collected all the data he could find on the Burr trial, but when he forwarded it to Congress he did not hint so broadly that impeachment was the remedy as he had in the Pickering and Chase cases. Albert J. Beveridge argues that Jefferson's annual message of October 27, 1807, urged the House to impeach Marshall. Jefferson asked Congress to decide whether the defect which led to Burr's acquittal was "in the testimony, in the law, or in the administration of the law; and wherever it shall be found, the Legislature alone can apply or originate the remedy." (In his first draft, Jefferson had the words "whether there is not a radical defect" before "in the administration of the law.") This can be interpreted as an invitation either to impeach the presiding judge or to amend the Constitution. He went on to say that if the present system does not adequately protect the government against destruction by treason, then "it is of importance to inquire by what means more effectual" such protection might be secured. This sounds more like a request for an amendment, which is how it was interpreted in Congress. Freshman Senator Edward Tiffin of Ohio offered a constitutional amendment to limit judicial independence only nine days after Jefferson's message had been read. The proposed amendment would have set a term of years (left blank in the proposal) for federal judges and would permit their removal by the President if requested by two-thirds of each house of Congress. Representative George W. Campbell of Tennessee moved an amendment in the House on January 30, 1808, which would require a three-fifths vote in each House for removal of a judge. This would lower the requirement only from 66⅔ percent in the Senate for removal, to 60 percent in each House; it would, however, dispense with the necessity of charging the judge with "high Crimes and Misdemeanors"—which was interpreted as an indictable offense—before impeaching and removing him. Several state legislatures passed resolutions urging even less protection for a judge. Pennsylvania and Virginia, for instance, favored removing federal judges on the request of a mere majority in each house of Congress. None of these proposals appear to have come to a vote in Congress.

ATTEMPTS TO LIMIT JUDICIAL TENURE

After the failure to remove Chase, Jefferson's policy changed drastically from the impeachment of judges to the limitation of their tenure. After 1805 his most frequent reference to impeachment was to describe it as "not even a scare-crow." The one time in later years when he again advocated impeachment, he urged a two-stage action by Congress. In 1821 he said that the judiciary's "unconstitutional invasions of state rights" should not result immediately in impeachment, but in a "strong protestation of both houses of Congress that such and such doctrines advanced by the supreme court, are contrary to the constitution: and if afterwards they relapse into the same heresies, impeach and set the whole adrift." Having forewarned the judges of the error of their ways, presumably Congress could then remove them with impunity.

More characteristic of Jefferson after the Chase affair was his proposal to establish limited, but renewable, terms for federal judges. In 1821 he proposed that judges serve "for six years (the Senatorial term) with a re-appointmentability by the president with the approbation of *both* houses." He regarded this as a high level of judicial independence, short only of the "total irresponsibility under which they are acting and sinning now." The next year he suggested that "future appointments of judges be for 4 to 6 years, and renewable by the President & Senate. This will bring their conduct, at regular periods, under revision and probation."

In both of these proposals, as in many other letters of this period, Jefferson observed that the American Constitution had opened the way to judicial tyranny by first copying and then far surpassing English judicial independence. While Jefferson agreed that judges should be independent of the executive, it was "of the first order of absurdity and inconsistence" for them to be beyond the control of the American people or their representatives. A similar doctrine had been preached by the Republican philosopher John Taylor of Caroline as early as 1801. Rather than rely on impeachments, Jefferson preferred the British system of making judges "removable on the joint address of both houses, by vote of a majority of each." Requiring a two-thirds vote would establish judges for life, as the "combination of the friends and associates of the accused, the action of personal and party passions, and the sympathies of the human heart, will for ever find means of influencing one third of either the one or the other house." Jefferson insisted that even the "habitual and maniac drunkard" Pickering would have held his bench if a real defense had been offered. Jefferson's criticisms of the too independent federal judiciary applied likewise to state judiciaries, which were established along similar lines.

The chance of having his commission renewed intermittently was to Jefferson all the independence that an honest and competent judge required. Although Julian Boyd describes Jefferson as "one who cherished the independence of the judiciary," the judges must have felt ravished rather than cherished when Jefferson turned his attention to the lifetime tenure (or "good behavior," which in practice meant the same thing) which contributed so much to their independence. In his dealings with British and French diplomats as secretary of state in 1793, Jefferson spoke proudly of the sacrosanct independence of the judiciary. "When either persons or property are taken into their custody," he loftily informed Edmond Charles Genêt, "there is no power in this country that can take them out." And in a 1776 letter attributed to Jefferson, which Boyd convincingly argues is "highly suspect," Jefferson is quoted as arguing that the minds of state judges "should not be *distracted with jarring interests;* they should not be *dependent upon any man or body of men.* To these ends they should hold *estates for life* in their offices, or, in other words, their commissions should be *during good behaviour,* and their salaries ascertained and established by law." If he were alleged to have written this after 1801, it would be not just "suspect," but absolutely incredible. One of Jefferson's greatest concerns in his later years was with judges' tenure in office, which he thought pushed them beyond independence to irresponsibility and eventually to tyranny.

Marshall indirectly answered Jefferson when a limited judicial tenure was considered during the Virginia Constitutional

Convention of 1829. Marshall could think of no evil more serious than to "destroy the tenure by which her judges hold their offices." Because the judiciary passes on every man's "property, his reputation, his life, his all," it is essential that the judge "be rendered perfectly and completely independent, with nothing to influence or controul him but God and his conscience."

JEFFERSONIAN JUSTICES

Jefferson also recognized, of course, that the safest method of republicanizing the judiciary was to make good Republican appointments. He had not been notably successful in his two appointments to the Supreme Court, for William Johnson and Brockholst Livingston joined the Marshall team more often than they disrupted it. But this did not prevent him from offering President Madison unsolicited advice about his own appointments. Jefferson became especially helpful in 1810 when he learned of the "opportune" death of Justice William Cushing and the imminent death of District Judge Cyrus Griffin of Virginia. Besides his pleasure at seeing Federalist judges leave the bench, even if it was feet first, Jefferson was inspired by a $100,000 suit just brought against him by Edward Livingston. It is significant that in his correspondence with Madison, Secretary of Treasury Albert Gallatin, and Attorney General Caesar A. Rodney, in which he advances the candidacy of John Tyler for the district court and Levi Lincoln for the Supreme Court, Jefferson turned immediately from his judicial recommendations to his personal judicial problem. While he was certain that justice was on his side, he had no confidence that Supreme Court *justices* would be! He gave this assessment of Chief Justice Marshall in a letter to Gallatin:

> the Judge's inveteracy is profound, and his mind of that gloomy malignity which will never let him forego the opportunity of

satiating it on a victim. his decisions, his instructions to a jury, his allowances & disallowances & garblings of evidence, must all be subjects of appeal. I consider that as my only chance of saving my fortune from entire wreck. and to whom is my appeal? from the judge in Burr's case to himself & his associate judges in the case of Marbury v. Madison.*

In May 1810 Jefferson rejoiced at the departure of "so wretched a fool" as Judge Griffin from the circuit court which would hear Livingston v. Jefferson, 15 Federal Cases 8411 (1811):

> really the state has suffered long enough by having such a cypher in so important an office, and infinitely the more from the want of any counterpoise to the rancorous hatred which Marshal bears to the government of his country, & from the cunning & sophistry within which he is able to enshroud himself. it will be difficult to find a character of firmness enough to preserve his independance on the same bench with Marshall.†

Four months later, Jefferson found Cushing's death a personal "godsend" because of the Livingston suit, and a national blessing because at last there was "a chance of getting a Republican majority in the supreme judiciary." Actually, there would be only an equality between Republicans and Federalists, but if Madison chose well he might finally end the Supreme Court's defiance of "the spirit & will of the nation."

Madison appointed both of the men recommended by Jefferson. Governor John Tyler, father of the President of the same name, became district judge in time to side with Jefferson in the trespass case of *Livington* v. *Jefferson* in circuit court in 1812. Levi Lincoln was appointed to the Supreme Court, as Jefferson had wished, but Lincoln declined because

---

* Jefferson to Gallatin, September 27, 1810, Library of Congress: Jefferson Papers.

† Jefferson to Madison, May 25, 1810, Library of Congress: Jefferson Papers.

of bad health and eyesight. Madison made several other attempts before finally coming to Joseph Story, who was regarded by Jefferson as a pseudo-Republican and a Loyalist.

LIVINGSTON V. JEFFERSON

The Tyler appointment at least solved Jefferson's immediate problem, because Tyler prevented Marshall from forwarding the suit against Jefferson to the Supreme Court. This suit involved Batture Ste. Marie, an area built up by Mississippi River siltage just south of New Orleans. Upon his arrival in New Orleans in 1804, Edward Livingston quickly became involved in litigation over this alluvial land, first as legal representative and then as part owner. First city officials and then Republican Governor William C. C. Claiborne denied that the batture was private property. When the territorial court ruled that it did not belong to the city, it was then asserted that it must be federal land. President Jefferson agreed, without hesitation or investigation, and in 1807 he ordered the United States marshal to eject the "intruders" who owned the batture. The emotional involvement of Jefferson in this case can only be ascribed to political prejudice against Livingston. Both in New York and Louisiana, Livingston had been too close to the proscribed Aaron Burr. The deprivation of a citizen's property by executive order was the subject of several pamphlets published by Livingston in 1807 and 1808. Jefferson issued a ninety-one page answer in 1810, shortly after Livingston filed suit for trespass against Jefferson in Richmond and against the United States marshal in New Orleans.

Although Jefferson said he wanted the case decided on its merits, he let his attorneys win its dismissal on a technicality— lack of jurisdiction. The English precedent was that "an action to recover damages for injuries to the land can be brought only where the land lies." Therefore, Jefferson could not be sued in circuit court in Richmond, and naturally he would not go to Louisiana in order to be sued. Tyler wrote Jefferson that Marshall would have forwarded the case to the Supreme Court "by adjournment or somehow or other" if Tyler had not "pressed the propriety" of its being decided in circuit court. In a written opinion strikingly reminiscent of *Marbury* v. *Madison,* Marshall lectured Jefferson but admitted that the circuit court in Virginia had no jurisdiction to hear the case. He thought it immoral to permit a technicality to prevent the hearing of a case in which "the injured party may have a clear right without a remedy." Marshall could not be blamed for indirectly chiding the former President for using "the common law of England" to claim nonjurisdiction, when Jefferson had so often attacked American judges for trying to sneak the common law into American judicature. But "this common law has been adopted by the legislature of Virginia," Marshall said; then he turned the knife by adding that even "had it not been adopted, I should [still] have thought it in force." In 1813 when the case *was* decided on its merits, Livingston's position was upheld. He won his case against the United States Marshal in the United States Court of Orleans District; the issues were the same, except that Jefferson's representative rather than Jefferson himself was the defendant, and the marshal *was* "where the land lies." Despite this victory, Livingston's family was involved in litigation regarding the Batture Ste. Marie for forty years longer.

Neither Jefferson nor Marshall ever forgave the other for his involvement in this case. Jefferson held Marshall himself partly responsible for the case. He insisted that it was "knolege of Marshall's character" which caused Livingston to bring suit. Marshall's "twistifications in the case of Marbury, in that of Burr, & the late Yazoo case shew how dexterously he can reconcile law to his own personal biasses." Marshall's contempt for Jefferson was likewise increased. He thought it hypocritical for a professed defender of civil liberties to take advantage of a technicality in order to evade a case involving a citizen's property rights. In 1821, when Jefferson's attacks on the Marshall Court were hot and heavy, Marshall remarked to Story that "The case of the mandamus may be the cloak, but the batture is recollected [by Jefferson] with still more resentment." "The Batture," he remarked two months later, "will never be forgotten" by Jefferson.

A series of events added fuel to the Jefferson-Marshall antagonism during the political decline of Jefferson and the judicial ascendancy of Marshall—from 1807 to 1826. First came the Aaron Burr treason trial in circuit court at Richmond in 1807. This was followed shortly by the completion of Marshall's *Life of George Washington,* which Jefferson regarded as a "party diatribe" and a "five volumed libel." From 1810 to 1812 Jefferson suffered through the batture crisis, which Marshall regarded as central to their mutual enmity. Marshall decisions of 1819, especially *McCulloch* v. *Maryland,* brought a new flurry of Jeffersonian criticism of the Supreme Court. Finally, the peak of anti-Marshallism came in 1821, in response to *Cohens* v. *Virginia.*

THE TREASON TRIAL OF AARON BURR

Since Edward S. Corwin established the practice in 1919, it has become fashionable to regard the acquittal of Aaron Burr as just one more proof of how far Marshall would go in order to embarrass President Jefferson politically. Corwin could comprehend Marshall's handling of the case only as another political coup. Too many historians who have dealt with the case since 1919 have not looked beyond Corwin. He regarded Marshall's handling of this case as "the one serious blemish on his judicial record." Yet Corwin did not contend that Burr was guilty. Even though Marshall permitted District Attorney George Hay remarkable leeway in the presentation of his evidence, he was not able to establish a convincing case against Burr—largely because the least reliable and most dishonorable participant in the trial was the principal witness for the prosecution, General James Wilkinson. There is no question that Aaron Burr had been up to something—perhaps to many things—in the West, but the prosecution did not demonstrate that it was dismemberment of the Union.

Corwin and most other historians attack Marshall for inconsistency in his interpretation of the treason clause, contending that he shifted from a less restrictive view of treason solely to embarrass the President. Marshall did not make it easy for the prosecution to prove that Burr was guilty of treason, but the framers of the Constitution had not intended for it to be easy. So many members of the Federal convention had, themselves, been in jeopardy of treason charges for their revolutionary activities if the British had succeeded in reclaiming the American Colonies, that it is not surprising that they made a conscious effort to make conviction for treason difficult. The Constitution provides that "Treason against the United States shall consist only in levying War against them, or in adhering to their Enemies, giving them Aid and Comfort. No Person shall be convicted of Treason unless on the Testimony of two Witnesses to the same overt Act, or on Confession in open Court."

When the prosecution could not prove that Burr had overtly levied war against the United States, Marshall stopped the arguments about peripheral issues and remanded the case to the jury, after instructing them at great length regarding the law of treason. His highly restrictive reading of the treason clause was one that under more normal circumstances—less politics and less emotionalism—should have delighted Thomas Jefferson for its protection of individual liberties. Even though several of the jurymen had admitted their prejudice against Burr before the trial, they had no option but to acquit him. As a parting shot at Marshall, they ruled that "Aaron Burr is not proved to be guilty under this indictment by any evi-

dence submitted to us. We therefore find him not guilty."
Marshall directed that this be recorded more prosaically as
"Not Guilty."

Marshall did not venture lightly or frivolously into the Burr
case. A month before the trial began he sought the advice of
the associate justices regarding all aspects of treason, though
he realized they would hesitate to comment on another judge's
case when they had not even heard the arguments. Because of
Marshall's laxness in preserving his correspondence, we cannot
know what, if anything, his associates recommended. After
the court had adjourned Marshall wrote Judge Richard Peters
that while the case was not taken seriously in Philadelphia, it
was "most deplorably serious" in Richmond. He thought it
"the most unpleasant case which has ever been brought before
a Judge in this, or, perhaps, in any other country which affected
to be governed by laws."

Fortunately Robert K. Faulkner's valuable recent study of
Marshall's philosophy has demonstrated conclusively that
Marshall was not guilty as charged of vacillating in his treatment of the treason clause. As alleged inconsistency is the
basis of the charge that Marshall was guilty of political bias
in the Burr trial, the charge should now be dropped, or new
and better evidence presented. Unfortunately, however, the
myth of Marshall's misconduct will probably persist; it has
outlived other recent studies of the Burr case which have
likewise exonerated Marshall. The longevity of this assumption about Marshall's misconduct is, perhaps, an inevitable
outgrowth of *Marbury* v. *Madison*. The deft political touch
demonstrated by Marshall in that first important decision has
led historians to expect the same in any other case in which
Thomas Jefferson was personally involved.

Marshall must have found political delight in the "neat
turning of the tables" which permitted him to test Republican
adherence to the judicial standards so recently demanded of
Justice Chase. Chase had been under attack by Republicans

for his oppressive conduct, for his adherence to the English common law interpretation of sedition, for his refusal to permit defense counsel to present their case, for ignoring state judicial procedures, and for angrily denying an appeal for a subpoena to force President John Adams to testify, thus seeming to put the Chief Executive above the law. Marshall carefully reversed each of these grounds of complaint, to the accompaniment of outraged cries from Jeffersonians who were now the prosecutors rather than the defenders. Even though he probably smiled at this Republican shift, this is no proof that Marshall's "turning of the tables" was politically motivated. He so thoroughly disapproved of Chase's conduct on the bench, that for Marshall to act like Chase would be far more astonishing than for him to behave as he did in the Burr case.

Faulkner reaches the intriguing conclusion that if Marshall was guilty of any bias it was *against* Burr. Burr and his associates thought so, of course, but even Marshall admitted that he set bail higher than was justified by his own "ideas of propriety." This, plus the wide latitude given to the prosecution, gives some credence to Burr's protest that Marshall sacrificed his principles in order "to conciliate Jack Cade" (the fifteenth-century English rebel who was regarded as the epitome of rabble-rousing democracy). Marshall's remark after the case that this "most unpleasant case" could have been less painful to himself if he had obeyed "the public will" indicates that he was aware of public sentiment regarding Burr and, therefore, of the threat Marshall would present to the judiciary if he brazenly flouted that sentiment. Marshall and the judiciary had nothing to gain politically by snatching Burr from under the Jefferson steam roller. In the popular mind, it was Marshall who emerged (with Burr) as the villain of this case, not Jefferson. William Branch Giles, for instance, referred to Marshall in the Senate, not by name but by implication, as a "miserable political intriguer, scrambling for power." Considering Burr's background, probably neither conviction nor acquittal represented perfect justice—but, considering the evidence presented in this case, acquittal came closer.

Besides his chief sin of preventing a jury that was eager to convict Burr from doing so, there were two other principal complaints against Marshall's handling of the case. First, he lectured the President again, as in *Marbury* v. *Madison*; and second, he subpoenaed the President, even though he had said in *Marbury* v. *Madison* that the President is "accountable only to his country in his political character and to his own conscience."

The remark that Jeffersonians found most offensive was not unwarranted. Marshall warned the grand jury that "the hand of malignity" must not be permitted to "grasp any individual against whom its hate may be directed or whom it may capriciously seize, charge him with some secret crime and put him on the proof of his innocence." This was widely interpreted as a personal attack on the President. Later Marshall insisted that he was only paraphrasing the British legal scholar, Blackstone, though citing this precedent did not lessen the sting. Besides, it approached the truth too closely. The extensive correspondence between President Jefferson and District Attorney George Hay clearly shows that the President was directing the prosecution from behind the scenes. Yet, at this same time, he piously informed an ally of Burr's who sought his aid that if the President were to interfere in a judicial case he would be subject to "just censure." Thus Marshall's remarks about the "hand of malignity" may have seemed too "just" for comfort.

Marshall was also criticized for not rebuking defense counsel for its frequent assaults upon the executive. William Wirt chided the court for listening "with all complacency" as Burr's counsel characterized the Jefferson administration as " 'blood hounds,' hunting this man with a keen and savage thirst for blood." In fairness to Marshall it should be noted that this was a remarkably freewheeling trial in which the prosecution also managed to work in some very strong language.

When he appeared before the grand jury, Burr asked Marshall to subpoena President Jefferson to force the presentation of certain letters to Jefferson and also governmental orders (which had been printed in the newspapers) calling for the destruction of Burr's "person and property." Alexander McRae argued for the prosecution that the President could not be forced to disclose "confidential communications," citing as precedent Marshall's decision regarding Attorney General Levi Lincoln's testimony during the *Marbury* trial.

Irving Brant, like Jefferson himself, regards Marshall's decision to subpoena Jefferson as "plainly designed to insult the President." Yet Marshall expressed "as guarded respect for the chief magistrate of the Union as is compatible with [the Court's] official duties." But it would "justly tarnish the reputation of the court," and perhaps of the United States government, if he permitted respect for the executive to cause the withholding of information needed by a defendant. Marshall did, indeed, subpoena the President, though he did it with utmost reluctance. He urged the prosecution to supply the papers voluntarily. He emphasized that if the President would send the papers there would be no need for him to appear in person. If the papers demanded were "state papers," this might justify their nondelivery. The belittling remarks about the President which Marshall is so often said to have made simply are not there, with the possible exception of his observation that "it is apparent" that the demand on Jefferson's time by executive duties "is not unremitting." Jefferson became extremely defensive, exploding from Washington that if Marshall was alluding to "our annual retirement from the seat of government during the sickly season, he should be told that ... I pass more hours in public business at Monticello than I do here everyday and it is much more laborious because all must be done in writing." Although Jefferson quite properly refused to appear in circuit court, he did submit the subpoenaed documents. Sixty years later the President was ruled by the Supreme Court to be immune from legal action.

A PARTISAN HISTORIAN

The Burr trial being finally ended, Jefferson turned his attention to the recently published fifth volume of Marshall's massive *Life of Washington*. As early as 1802, before any of the work was in print, Jefferson had begun to worry about Marshall the historian. He was sure that the biography had been written solely for "electioneering purposes" and would, therefore, be rushed into print in time to influence the presidential election of 1804. The early Marshall volumes were more likely to put readers to bed than to drive them to the polls, however. The first two volumes are a colonial history in which even George Washington scarcely makes an appearance. The next two volumes deal with the Revolution, which was not a major issue between Federalists and Republicans. Volume Five would cover the Washington administrations and the founding of the Republican party, and from it Jefferson expected the worst.

When he completed the volume in the summer of 1806, Marshall anticipated untrue charges and unmerited abuse. He wrote John Adams that "the imprudent task I have just executed will draw upon me a degree of odium & calumny which I might perhaps otherwise have escaped." He said that he tried to avoid "unnecessarily wounding the dominant party" in his treatment of the "turbulent and factious" 1790s, but the truth would offend some Jeffersonians.

Foremost among the offended was Thomas Jefferson. In 1802 Jefferson tried to persuade poet Joel Barlow to write a Republican "history of the United States, from the close of the War downwards," to counter Marshall's "party diatribe."

He offered Barlow the use of government documents and his own and Madison's personal recollections as resources. Seven years later he was still prodding Barlow, even though Jefferson himself still had not forwarded the promised documents. Then the President began reading Marshall's fifth volume to "correct what is wrong in it, and commit to writing such facts and annotations as the reading of that work will bring into my recollection, and which have not yet been put on paper." When Barlow became minister to France, Jefferson demanded to know what would become of "the antidotes of truth to the misrepresentations of Marshall." This "book" died with its "author" in the snows of Poland, where Barlow had followed Napoleon in 1812.

The "antidotes of truth," or often anecdotes, which were collected to refute Marshall's *Washington,* became the basis of Jefferson's famous "Anas," his memoranda regarding the politics of the 1790s. In his introduction to the "Anas," Jefferson states that many of the notes would not have been preserved but for the necessity of defending himself and his policies against the Marshall history. Jefferson charged that Marshall "culled" from Washington's paper a history as different from what Washington himself would have written "as was the candor of the two characters [Washington and Marshall] during the period of the war." After reading Jefferson's assault on John Marshall the historian, it is a letdown to learn how picayune and trivial most of his refutations of Volume Five really are.

When Jefferson wrote to John Adams regarding Marshall's "libels," Adams responded with an apt description of Marshall's *Washington.* He likened it to the Washington monument then being planned; the biography was "a Mausolaeum, 100 feet square at the base, and 200 feet high." Adams would have been happier if the principal theme of Marshall's last volume had been the evil influence of Alexander Hamilton, but this would have been a book written more likely by Joel Barlow than John Marshall. Adams anticipated that his own administration would have "no Character at all" in future histories because of "the impious Idolatry to Washington" in histories like Marshall's.

RENEWED JEFFERSONIAN ASSAULTS ON THE MARSHALL COURT

Major Supreme Court decisions in 1819 and 1821—most notably *McCulloch* v. *Maryland* and *Cohens* v. *Virginia*—led to a major Jeffersonian revulsion against the Court. Publicly, the leaders were Judge Spencer Roane of the Virginia Supreme Court of Appeals and John Taylor of Caroline. Roane is generally assumed to have been in line for the chief justiceship if Adams and Marshall had not beaten Jefferson to the nomination in 1801. Taylor, the philosopher of Jeffersonian Republicanism, virtually disowned Presidents Jefferson and Madison when political necessities forced them to stray from Virginia Republicanism as preached in Caroline County. During their administrations Taylor regarded them as nationalist and broad construction apostates. Although Jefferson confined his attacks on the Marshall Court largely to private letters, he encouraged and praised Roane and Taylor and anyone else who would take on Marshall publicly. Jefferson generally insisted that his letters on the judiciary be kept confidential; nevertheless, enough came into print to convince Justice Joseph Story— still officially a Republican but primarily a disciple of John Marshall—that "Mr. Jefferson stands at the head of the enemies of the Judiciary." Story felt that the only support for the judiciary would come from "the wise and the good and the elevated in society." He was certain in 1822 that Jefferson had no place in this select group.

From 1819 to 1825 (only a half-year before his death), Jefferson wrote letter after letter warning that the Supreme Court was the "engine of consolidation" or the "germ that is

to destroy" the Federal balance between state and central
authority. He said that Marshall and his cohorts treated the
Constitution as "a mere thing of wax . . . which they may twist
and shape into any form they please." The Court was the
more "sure and deadly" because it was "seemingly passive and
unassuming." Jefferson varied his metaphors in describing the
judiciary in this period, but he invariably stressed its stealth.
Apparently his favorite image, as he used it in letters written
in 1820, 1823, and 1825 and in the "Autobiography" which he
wrote in 1821, was to treat the judges as covert enemies under-
mining the Constitution by tunneling beneath it: "The judiciary of the US. is the subtle corps of sappers & miners constantly working under ground to undermine the foundations
of our confederated fabric." Another favorite metaphor was
to compare the advance of the Court to the unobserved force
of gravity. He improved on this one each time he used it in
1821, so that by August the judiciary was both a thief and an
irresistible force. It worked "like gravity by night and by day,
gaining a little to-day and a little tomorrow, and advancing
its noiseless step like a thief, over the field of jurisdiction,
until all shall be usurped from the states, & the government
of all be consolidated into one." Jefferson also took frequent
pleasure in reminding his correspondents of the "peculiar
maxim and creed" of judges that "it is the office of a good
judge to enlarge his jurisdiction."

From 1821 to 1823 Jefferson waged his campaign to force
the Supreme Court to return to seriatim decisions, so that each
justice would be required to justify his own reasons for a
decision. This would lessen the judges' opportunities for
stealth by making their mental processes more visible than
when they are "cooking up opinions in conclave." Besides
urging Justice William Johnson to resume individual decisions, Jefferson also asked Madison to see if he could likewise
influence Justices Duval and Todd.

By 1825 Jefferson seems to have conceded victory to

Marshall. In March he disgustedly described the central government as "our foreign department," and in December he wrote that the "federal branch of our government," not just the judiciary, was usurping all the rights of the states. By then the executive (John Quincy Adams) and Congress seemed to him to be competing with the judiciary in the race to weaken the states. Yet when Marshall died a decade later, he was deeply frustrated because of Congress' failure to use the power authorized by his decisions. He had opened the doorway to national authority, but Congress had not gone through it.

MARSHALL'S COUNTERATTACK

Considering the extent of Jeffersonian assaults on John Marshall and his Court, Marshall made surprisingly little counterattack. His hands and thoughts were not as clean as he professed in 1832, though, when he said he had "never allowed myself to be irritated by Mr. Jefferson's unprovoked and unjustified aspersions on my conduct and principles." He added that he had never even *noticed* them—probably he meant public notice—except once during the XYZ affair, when failure to reply would imply that he was "crouching under the lash, and admitting the justice of its infliction." His biographer, Beveridge, asserts that "Marshall did not express the intensity of his feeling" about Jefferson because he "had no stomach for verbal encounters. . . . Personal warfare by tongue or pen was beyond or beneath him. Marshall simply could not scold or browbeat. He was incapable of participating in a brawl." Beveridge's implication was that Jefferson reveled in all these activities which Marshall disdained.

Yet Marshall's extensive correspondence with Joseph Story demonstrates that he not only noticed Jefferson's aspersions but was sometimes stung by them. The letters hint at what Marshall must have been saying about Jefferson to those other

justices who were susceptible to Jefferson-baiting. His surviving counterattacks against Jefferson and Jeffersonian Virginia were bunched in 1819 and 1821, the years in which he
was under heaviest attack, and in 1830 to 1833, at the height of
the nullification crisis. When Story wrote in 1821 that Jefferson wanted to prostrate the judiciary and destroy public
respect for it, Marshall replied that he was grieved rather than
surprised. He regarded Jefferson as "among the most ambi-
tious, & I suspect among the most unforgiving of men."
Because Jefferson's influence rested upon democracy, he resented any check which the judiciary might apply to the
masses' "wild impulse of the moment." Marshall lumped
Jefferson among those whose "judgement is completely con-
trouled by the passions." Marshall was especially outraged
by the "coarseness & malignity" of Spencer Roane's "Algernon
Sidney" essays against the Supreme Court and the *Cohens*
decision. Marshall thought that no one but Roane could use
such coarse language, but "its acerbity had been increased by
his communications with the great Lama of the mountains."
This nickname for Jefferson was apparently common with
Marshall, as was his practice of saying "Tom Jefferson?" as
if the democratic leader's reputation was a question which
would be answered differently by future generations. Whereas
scolding or haranguing did not come easily to Marshall, humor
and playfulness did, so he probably had a variety of other
ways of twitting Jefferson without really saying anything
explicit against him. It should be added that Jefferson was a
meticulous preserver of correspondence, so whatever he said
about Marshall is preserved. Marshall, on the other hand, was
a slovenly record keeper, so the Marshall side of the debate
probably seems scantier than it really was.

Just as the publication of Marshall's *Life of Washington*
had prompted an angry counterattack by Jefferson, the edition
of Jefferson's correspondence published in 1829 was read by
Marshall "with astonishment and deep felt disgust." Marshall

was so bitter about Jefferson's "repeated unwarrantable aspersions on my self" that he considered publishing a self-defense,
but "age has blunted my feelings." Besides, the facts were
already available for anyone with a fair mind, and nothing
he could say would persuade the unfair. He added that "nothing is unknown or can be misunderstood by intelligent men
unless it be the motives which compelled the court to give its
opinion at large on the case of Marbury vs Madison." Regrettably, he does not expand upon that tantalizing remark.

MARSHALL'S RELATIONSHIP WITH VIRGINIA

Marshall's relationship with his—but mainly Jefferson's—
state of Virginia was uncomfortable for both sides. Marshall
was liked almost everywhere that he was known personally,
but outside of Richmond he was known largely through the
Republican press. His cordiality and modesty made him a
walking disproof in Richmond of the Republican doctrine
that Federalists were haughty monarchists. When a convention
was chosen to revise the Virginia constitution, Marshall was
the overwhelming choice of the Richmond district. Richmond,
however, had long remained a haven of Federalism in Republican Virginia. This made life more tolerable for Marshall,
but it may be that the simple republican mannerisms of
Marshall made Federalism more tolerable for Richmond.

As early as 1796, when Jefferson sought and lost the presidency, Marshall was already disgusted with the politics of the
rest of Virginia. He wrote Justice James Iredell that he hoped
North Carolina would not "head the crooked paths of Virginia." After becoming chief justice, however, Marshall said
little against his state except in 1819 (after *McCulloch* v.
Maryland), in 1821 (after *Cohens* v. *Virginia*), and in 1832–
1833 (during the nullification crisis). A month after
McCulloch v. *Maryland* he warned Story that the decision had
"roused the sleeping spirit of Virginia, if indeed it ever

sleeps." He expected the decision to be attacked unfairly but successfully, because the Virginia press was closed to anyone who supported the Supreme Court. Marshall justly complained to Justice Washington that the Republican legislature and executive who established the Bank of the United States would suffer no blame, "while the poor court who have nothing to give & of whom nobody is afraid bears all the obloquy of the measure." Although many critics of the Court were not angry at it for upholding the Bank, which was after all the off-spring of James Madison and John C. Calhoun, they hated the nationalistic language used in reaching the decision. Because no one else would defend the Court, Marshall, as "A Friend of the Union," wrote a counterattack against Roane, which Justice Washington placed in a Philadelphia newspaper on April 28 and May 1. "A Friend of the Union" attacked "those unfounded jealousies" of the central government which were regaining strength in Virginia. In June Marshall was working on a new series, "A Constitutionalist."

Marshall's 1821 challenge to Virginia, *Cohens* v. *Virginia,* went far beyond *Marbury* v. *Madison* in establishing judicial power. Because it also involved the Old Dominion and Judge Spencer Roane's court directly, Roane exceeded the invective of 1819. Marshall regarded this "champion of dismemberment" with greater contempt than he did any other Jeffersonian. He thought that Roane, and through him Jefferson, was seeking "to convert our government into a mere league of states." The assault against the powerless judiciary he regarded as a prelude to an attack on the entire central government. He insisted that Roane was "obviously approved & guided" in this by Thomas Jefferson.

Marshall also saw Jefferson's hand in the great crisis of the Jacksonian era. When South Carolina nullified the Tariff of 1832 and implied that it would secede from the Union if the United States government attempted to collect the tariff, Marshall regarded this as a natural but hideous outgrowth of the

Jeffersonian philosophy which had for so long prevailed in Virginia and the rest of the South. Early in August 1832, Marshall was optimistic that neither Virginia nor North Carolina would follow South Carolina if it persisted in its course; by September 22 he was coming "slowly and reluctantly to the conviction that our constitution cannot last." The miracles which had so far preserved the Union could not be expected to continue indefinitely. Even after the immediate crisis had ended, thanks to Henry Clay's compromise tariff of 1833, Marshall continued to fear that the South was "so far gone in political metaphysics" that not even Story's brilliant *Commentaries on the Constitution* could "restore us to common sense."

For the seemingly hopeless crisis that the United States faced as Marshall's judicial career ended, he blamed Thomas Jefferson and the state of Virginia. As he anxiously awaited word from the South Carolina convention which was in the process of nullifying federal legislation, Marshall cried, "We are now gathering the bitter fruits of the tree even before that time planted by Mr. Jefferson, and so industriously and perseveringly cultivated by Virginia." Thus continued the debate of John Marshall and Thomas Jefferson regarding the meaning of the Union and the functions of the judiciary—six years after Jefferson had left this life and only three years before Marshall would follow him.

⋙ 10 ⋘

MARBURY SINCE MARSHALL

The issues involved in the *Marbury* case were minor. Whether three minor individuals attained the minor offices to which they aspired was of little concern to the United States or even to Marbury, Ramsay, and Hooe. Moreover, Marshall's decision was faulty, even though it was politically brilliant. Discussed at great length in the decision were issues which the Court itself decided were not within its jurisdiction. The Supreme Court—even the Marshall Court—has overruled or ignored considerable parts of it. Even Marshall's brief for judicial review is persuasive primarily to persons who were already convinced that courts should determine the constitutionality of legislation. Yet *Marbury* v. *Madison* is by all odds the best known early decision of the United States judiciary. Even today it is probably surpassed in public recognition only by Brown v. Board of Education of Topeka, 347 U.S. 483 (1954). Constitutional lawyers and historians hold it in similar esteem; Leo Pfeffer, no admirer of Marshall or of *Marbury*, goes so far as to-estimate that "nine out of ten" would name

Marbury v. *Madison* without hesitation as "the most important decision in the history of the Supreme Court." If so, the Marshall decision is important primarily for what this slim entering wedge of judicial review has enabled later judges to do.

MARBURY AND THE CONSTITUTION

Marshall's decision earned such distinction not by being original or revolutionary, but by saying what so many contemporary lawyers and legislators had already taken for granted. There is an important link here between the Marshall of *Marbury* v. *Madison* and the Jefferson of the Declaration of Independence. Even though he was writing a document intended to rationalize revolution, Jefferson did not use revolutionary ideas. Like Marshall in 1803, he stated what concerned Americans apparently regarded as common sense. Neither the Declaration of Independence nor the *Marbury* doctrine of judicial review caused great controversy because each stated arguments which the American people were prepared to accept.

The intentions of the framers of the Constitution regarding the manner of interpreting and enforcing the "higher law" which they were creating are constantly debated. The more prolific Founding Fathers seemed to favor some sort of judicial review, but it is likely that most of them thought that judicial review would be confined to blatant violations of the Constitution. Because Congress is as capable of recognizing and rejecting obviously unconstitutional legislation as the Supreme Court, the significant judicial review cases have been based on fine (sometimes strained) distinctions—such as the voiding of Section 13 of the Judiciary Act of 1789. This "unconstitutional" law is more typical of the legislation which has since been invalidated by the Supreme Court than are the hypothetical examples so self-righteously advanced by Marshall in *Marbury* v. *Madison*. Marshall was, of course, correct when he argued that duties on exports, bills of attainder, ex post facto laws, or laws changing the requirements for conviction of treason were so obviously unconstitutional that they *must* be void. They were also so obviously unconstitutional that Congress has not passed legislation which clearly violated these restrictions.

EARLY USE OF JUDICIAL REVIEW

Whatever the intentions of the framers of the Constitution, judicial review had been practiced frequently by both state and federal courts in the fourteen years after the establishment of the Constitution. State courts were engaged in interpreting both the United States Constitution and their individual state constitutions. Although there was grumbling by the parties adversely affected by such decisions, no concerted nationwide opposition had developed. Madison's Virginia Resolutions and Jefferson's Kentucky Resolutions of 1798, for instance, declared the Alien and Sedition Acts unconstitutional and advanced the states as proper interpreters of the Constitution. Northern legislatures replied, however, that the Supreme Court was the final interpreter of the Constitution. Madison came close to agreeing in his 1799 Report, which was adopted by the Virginia General Assembly. Jefferson probably would have concurred if the Supreme Court had "proved itself" by voiding the hated Alien and Sedition Acts rather than enforcing them. Again in 1819, Jefferson's displeasure with the Supreme Court surely would have been mollified had the Court used its judicial power to destroy the Bank of the United States rather than justify it.

The judiciary was relatively safe so long as it was the outcome of specific cases which delighted or outraged statesmen and lawyers. The danger would come if large numbers of these statesmen and lawyers were to protest the judiciary's self-proclaimed role as final interpreter of the Constitution, whether the decision was for them or against them. In 1807 Jefferson was angered to find the prosecution in the Burr trial, and even his own attorney general, citing *Marbury* v. *Madison* as a precedent to meet their needs of the moment. How much more painful it must have been, if he noticed it, to see even Spencer Roane using the *Marbury* precedent to justify judicial review. Roane declared Section 25 of the Judiciary Act of 1789 unconstitutional in Hunter v. Martin, 4 Munford 3 (1815), a case in the Virginia Supreme Court of Appeals which involved the Fairfax estate. Roane remarked that another part of this "hurried" Judiciary Act had already been "detected and admitted by the Supreme Court of the United States itself, in the case of *Marbury* v. *Madison*," to be unconstitutional. If the devil can quote Scripture, then Spencer Roane can quote John Marshall! Roane would have stripped much authority from the federal judiciary and government if he had succeeded in voiding Section 25, for it gave the United States Supreme Court the authority to hear cases on appeals from the highest state courts. This section came as close as Congress ever would to authorizing the exercise of judicial review by federal and state courts. In a kind of parody of *Marbury* v. *Madison,* Roane was using judicial review to strip the Supreme Court of important jurisdiction; Marshall had denied his Court trivial jurisdiction while establishing the important precedent of judicial review. Joseph Story in Martin v. Hunter's Lessee, 1 Wheaton 304 (1816), and Marshall in *Cohens* v. *Virginia* successfully refuted Roane's ideas on Supreme Court jurisdiction. Marshall did not participate in the *Martin* case because of his financial involvement in its outcome. Story probably protected Marshall's pecuniary interests more completely than Marshall would have dared to do.

Roane attempted to use *Marbury* v. *Madison* rather than cast it into the void. So, also, have later generations been more concerned about how it is used rather than whether it should be. Liberals who would have opposed judicial review in the economic decision era of Van Devanter and McReynolds decided in the civil liberties decision age of Warren, Black, and Douglas that it is not so bad after all. As the Burger era begins, conservatives look to new uses of judicial review rather than its cessation. The United States Chamber of Commerce, for instance, is already eagerly anticipating the return of economic decisions to a prominence which they have not had since 1937. It has resented the manner in which the judiciary of the past three decades has avoided the voiding of regulations on the economy.

So long as Americans drift back and forth between admiring and disdaining judicial review, rather than settling permanently in the critics' camp, *Marbury* v. *Madison* will be revered as the first decision which invalidated federal legislation and the first decision to deal in some depth with the judiciary's role as interpreter of the Constitution. Congressmen had advanced similar arguments during the repeal debates of 1802, but they were many voices, not one as the Supreme Court was in 1803. John Marshall might have offered the same views if he had remained in Congress, but the voice of Representative Marshall would have been muted compared with the voice of Chief Justice Marshall.

JUSTICE GIBSON REFUTES *MARBURY* V. *MADISON*

With even Spencer Roane, Marshall's bitterest political and personal enemy, using judicial review rather than abusing it, it is not surprising that a generation passed before *Marbury* v. *Madison* was answered in detail. By 1825, when Justice John B. Gibson of the Pennsylvania Supreme Court undertook a refutation of Marshall in *Eakin* v. *Raub,* he complained that judicial review had become "a professional dogma" resting on faith rather than reason. Gibson himself had been a believer in judicial review until he examined it more closely. He could find no judge besides Marshall in *Marbury* v. *Madison* who had ventured even to discuss this doctrine which all seemed to take for granted. While William Paterson had advanced some "beautiful figures" to justify voiding Pennsylvania legislation in *Van Horne's Lessee* v. *Dorrance* (1795), Gibson insisted that "metaphorical illustration is one thing and argument another." Even Marshall took for granted "the very thing to be proved"—that the judiciary has authority to judge conflicts between the Constitution and normal legislation. Judicial review must be justified—if at all—on "the principles of the Constitution." When Gibson found that even John Marshall could not persuade him that the judiciary was the proper judge of the constitutionality of legislation, he concluded that it must be due to "the weakness of the position which he attempts to defend."

Gibson distinguished sharply between political and civil powers and insisted that the judiciary be confined to the latter. Since the Constitution, federal or state, is the most political of all legislation, it must be interpreted by legislatures rather than judiciaries. Gibson did not share the fear of legislative supremacy which underlay the *Marbury* decision. To him both executive and judiciary were subordinate to the legislature. Even if they were equal, the legislature would still be the best judge of the constitutionality of its own laws, as legislative acts are entitled to at least as much respect as judicial or executive acts.

It has been suggested that if Marshall had been confronted in the *Marbury* trial with an argument comparable to Gibson's he would have been compelled to give "a far higher exhibition of his powers than the case now affords." Marshall's argument probably would have been sharpened by hearing Gibson's views, but no lawyer—certainly not Charles Lee or Levi Lincoln or John B. Gibson—could have guessed beforehand that judicial review was even at issue in *Marbury* v. *Madison*. Even in Stuart v. Laird, where judicial review was anticipated as the major issue, counsel argued only against its propriety in that case, not against the theory of judicial review itself.

Gibson did not succeed in turning his contemporaries against judicial review. He did not even sway the Pennsylvania Supreme Court, for his *Eakin* decision was a dissent. The more typical attitude of that generation was expressed in the eulogy of Marshall delivered by Rufus Choate, one of the great lawyers of that time. Choate could think of nothing in American political history which outranked the *Marbury* decision. It was "an achievement of statesmanship of which a thousand years may not exhaust or reveal all the good." Even Gibson eventually backed away from criticizing *Marbury* v. *Madison*. He was chief justice of the Pennsylvania Supreme Court in 1846 when he heard *Eakin* v. *Raub* cited as precedent. He broke in to explain that he had "changed that opinion" because the recent state constitutional convention had by silence sanctioned judicial review and he had become convinced by experience of its necessity. Gibson's refutation of judicial review was not really "discovered" until the end of the nineteenth century, when it was popularized by Professor James Bradley Thayer of Harvard University, the patron saint of critics of judicial review. Thayer and *Eakin* have been as influential to advocates of judicial restraint—such as Oliver Wendell Holmes, Louis D. Brandeis, Felix Frankfurter, and Learned Hand—as Marshall and *Marbury* have been to the judicial activists.

MARSHALL-*MARBURY* IDOLATRY

Thayer and Holmes resumed the criticism of *Marbury* v. *Madison* at a time when the decision had gained almost religious acceptance among lawyers because it said just what they wanted to hear. A half-century passed between the first and second federal laws which were invalidated by the Supreme Court, but, during the period of economic boom which followed the Civil War, judicial intervention with federal legislation became a frequent occurrence. Furthermore, the voiding of state legislation was almost an everyday occurrence. Naturally, the corporation lawyers who dominated the American bar welcomed the protection which the various courts were extending, to their clients, and they revered the *Marbury* precedent which underlay this protection. The various celebrations in 1901 of the centennial of John Marshall's appointment worshiped John Marshall and judicial review as one. The three-volume set of centennial addresses devoted nearly twice as much attention to *Marbury* v. *Madison* as to the vitally important *McCulloch* v. *Maryland*, *Cohens* v. *Virginia*, or *Gibbons* v. *Ogden*.

Some of the speakers on Marshall implied that there must perforce be another centennial in 1903 to celebrate *Marbury* v. *Madison* properly. This decision was "an epoch in the world's history!" to the Georgia eulogist Burton Smith. It was "a bulwark of liberty and civilization, towering above all others erected by the Anglo-Saxon race!" Judge U. M. Rose of Arkansas, the major speaker in the Colorado ceremony, was slightly more restrained. He thought that "next to the formation of our government the decision in *Marbury* v. *Madison* is perhaps the most important event in our history." Without this decision the United States would have "neither unity, harmony nor perpetuity." In Oregon Horace G. Platt said the *Marbury* decision was "as great a document as the Bill of Rights, as far-reaching as the Declaration of Independence, as essential to the healthy development of our government under the Constitution as the Constitution itself." It was sporting of Platt to include Jefferson's Declaration of Independence, for 1901 was also the centennial of Jefferson's advancement to the presidency. Obviously Harvard Law Professor Jeremiah Smith did not agree with his colleague, Thayer. Smith said in New Hampshire that "if an addition is ever made to the number of days celebrated as national anniversaries, I submit that the twenty-fourth of February may well be added to the list." After compiling such praise, what could the editor of the centennial volumes, John F.

Dillon, possibly add in his introduction? He contented himself by merely describing *Marbury* v. *Madison* as "a new charter of individual rights and liberties."

JUDICIAL REVIEW IN THE TWENTIETH CENTURY

This idolatry did not survive in the twentieth century. Critical scholars and judges scrutinized *Marbury* from every angle to prove that Judge Learned Hand was correct in saying "it will not bear scrutiny." The decision blatantly violated the elementary rule that courts should seek a constitutional interpretation of legislation rather than an unconstitutional reading. There was no need, other than politics, for judicial review to have occurred in this case. Worse yet, Marshall's argument assumes, rather than demonstrates, the legitimacy of the Supreme Court's role as final interpreter of the Constitution. One of the earliest comprehensive critics of the *Marbury* decision, J. A. C. Grant, concluded grudgingly that all that remained was "its influence upon the development of our system of constitutional law." But that is immense! Deservedly or not, *Marbury* v. *Madison* has become the foundation of a judicial system that is unique in its power and influence.

The one man who has been proposed as a contender for Marshall's title as "the Great Chief Justice" takes more of an "old-time" view of the decision than many contemporary critics. Earl Warren, who has used judicial review and judicial activism with such tremendous impact in the middle of the twentieth century, singled out the establishment of judicial review in *Marbury* v. *Madison* as Marshall's greatest achievement. Warren was praising this decision not for what it was in 1803 but for what it had become in a century and a half. Right or not, flawed or not, *Marbury* v. *Madison* has become the symbol of American judicial review and, indeed, of the

American judiciary. How long it will survive, with all its contemporary flaws and latter-day achievements, will depend on the use which judges of the future will make of the power for which *Marbury* v. *Madison* has been the rationalization and symbol.

✑ Bibliographical Essay ℘

The starting point for any study of John Marshall and the Marshall Court is still Albert J. Beveridge's *The Life of John Marshall*, 4 vols. (Boston: Houghton Mifflin, 1916–1919), even though it has been in print for more than a half-century. Every page votes for Marshall and for Federalism, but for the reader who remains alert to this pitfall, this work is a mine of valuable information. Beveridge's massive biography has virtually preempted the field. The best short biography is of the same vintage. Like most other Marshall biographies, Edward S. Corwin's *John Marshall and the Constitution: A Chronicle of the Supreme Court* (New Haven, Conn.: Yale University Press, 1919) is really a history of his judicial career rather than a full biography. Charles Warren's *The Supreme Court in United States History*, 2 vols. (Boston: Little, Brown, 1926) has a wider scope than Beveridge's *Marshall,* but it adopts the same pro-Marshall, pro-Court, pro-Federalist view. Warren's work is so valuable a source of contemporary comments, especially from newspapers and congressional debates, that it is regrettable that it is not more accurate in its transcriptions. The one recent book which belongs among these essential aids to an understanding of Marshall is Robert Kenneth Faulkner's *The Jurisprudence of John Marshall* (Princeton, N.J.: Princeton University Press, 1968), a splendid index to the philosophy, as well as jurisprudence of John Marshall.

Three helpful political-judicial studies of "the great Chief Justice," the emphasis of each being revealed in the title, are David G. Loth's *Chief Justice: John Marshall and the Growth of the Republic* (New York: Norton, 1949); Samuel J. Konefsky's *John Marshall and Alexander Hamilton, Architects of the American Constitution* (New York: Macmillan, 1964); and Benjamin W. Palmer's *Marshall and Taney: Statesmen of the Law* (Minneapolis: University of Minnesota Press, 1939). Volumes that are collections of shorter essays on Marshall are Erwin C. Surrency's *The Marshall Reader* (New York: Oceana, 1955) and W. Melville Jones' *Chief Justice John Marshall: A Reappraisal* (Ithaca, N.Y.: Cornell University Press, 1956); the latter is a collection of addresses commemorating the two hundredth anniversary of Marshall's birth. Fortunately, these are more scholarly and critical than the 1,600 pages of hagiography commemorating the hundredth anniversary of Marshall's chief justiceship, which was edited by John F. Dillon in *John Marshall: Life, Character and Judicial Services* . . . , 3 vols. (Chicago: Callahan & Co., 1903) .

Aside from a quantity of judicial opinions and his large biography of George Washington, little that was written by Marshall is in print. The most important printed collection is "Letters of Chief Justice Marshall" edited by Charles C. Smith in the *Proceedings of the Massachusetts Historical Society*, 2d ser., XIV (1900) , 320–360. This is a valuable collection of letters written by Marshall to Associate Justice Joseph Story. Charles Warren helpfully supplied the other end of the correspondence in "The Story-Marshall Correspondence (1819–1831)," *William and Mary Quarterly*, 2d ser., XXI (1941), 1–26. John Edward Oster's *The Political and Economic Doctrines of John Marshall* . . . (New York: Neale Publishing Co., 1914; republished in 1967 by Burt Franklin) presents a wide variety of Marshall letters but is unreliable because of sloppy editing. It is extremely difficult to use because there is no discernible pattern or logic to the book. The Chief Justice's home life is glimpsed in "Letters from John Marshall to his Wife," *William and Mary Quarterly*, 2d ser., III (1923) , 73–90, and in Frances Norton Mason's excessively romantic *My Dearest Polly: Letters of Chief Justice John Marshall to His Wife* (Richmond, Va.: Garrett & Massie, 1961). There are some significant political letters in Jack L. Cross' "John Marshall on the French Revolution and on American Politics," *William and Mary Quarterly*, 2d ser., XII (1955), 631–649. John Stokes Adams edited *An Autobiographical Sketch by John Marshall* (Ann Arbor: University of Michigan Press, 1937) , a letter in which Marshall too briefly describes his life up to his appointment as chief justice. In time, all of this, and much more, will be available in *The Papers of John Marshall*, a definitive edition which is proceeding under the editorship of Stephen G. Kurtz at the Institute of Early American History and Culture; publication will begin in 1971 or 1972. Even after its publication large gaps will remain, however, because Marshall was not as outstanding a correspondent as Jefferson, Madison, or John Adams and he was, moreover, an outstandingly bad preserver of personal correspondence.

Marbury v. *Madison* has been taken for granted by historians almost as much as by judges and lawyers. Although virtually every book on the American judiciary mentions the case, remarkably few studies have concentrated on it. Edward S. Corwin studied it in depth in a chapter in *The Doctrine of Judicial Review* (Princeton, N.J.: Princeton University Press, 1914). J. A. C. Grant wrote a devastating criticism of the case in "Marbury v. Madison Today," *American Political Science Review,* XXIII (1929), 673–681, finding the decision wanting in almost every respect. Justice Harold H. Burton came to its defense in "The Cornerstone of Constitutional Law: The Extraordinary Case of Marbury v. Madison," *American Bar Association Journal,* XXXVI (October 1950), 805–808, 881–883. There is an entertaining account of the case in Joseph A. Garraty's *Quarrels That Have Shaped the Constitution* (New York: Harper, 1964). James B. Thayer's *John Marshall* (Boston: Houghton Mifflin, 1901) is one of the first reputable works to look with disfavor on judicial review. Louis B. Boudin's *Government by Judiciary,* 2 vols. (New York: William Godwin, Inc., 1932), regards *Marbury v. Madison* as he does every other exercise of judicial power—as an illicit intrusion. Occupying the middle ground between the extremes of Boudin and of Beveridge-Warren is Charles G. Haines' *The Role of the Supreme Court in American Government and Politics, 1789–1835* (Berkeley: University of California Press, 1944). Haines finds merit in Jefferson's judicial policies without going to the anti-Marshall extremes of Boudin. Leonard W. Levy has edited *Judicial Review and the Supreme Court* (New York: Harper, 1967), a useful collection of essays which place more emphasis than is customary on the undemocratic aspect of judicial review. Robert G. McCloskey's *The American Supreme Court* (Chicago: University of Chicago Press, 1960) is a brief and highly provocative history.

Kathryn Turner has published two fine articles on the period of Marshall's transition from politics to jurisprudence, "The Midnight Judges," *University of Pennsylvania Law Review,* CIX (1960–1961), 494–523, and "The Appointment of Chief Justice Marshall," *William and Mary Quarterly,* 3d ser., XVII (1960), 143–163. Charles S. Bundy's "A History of the Office of Justice of the Peace in the District of Columbia," *Records of the Columbia Historical Society,* V (1902), 259–293, is also helpful. Max Lerner's "John Marshall and the Campaign of History," *Columbia Law Review,* XXXIX (1939), 396–431, treats Marshall as practically an economic royalist.

Jefferson's side of the controversy is presented most accurately in Paul Leicester Ford's, *The Writings of Thomas Jefferson,* 10 vols. (New York: Putnam, 1892–1899). Eventually this will be superseded by Julian Boyd's *The Papers of Thomas Jefferson,* 17 vols. to date (Princeton, N.J.: Princeton University Press, 1950——), but since this huge project has reached only the early 1790s, it will be years before John Marshall and his Court become an important factor in the published *Papers.*

INDEX

ABOUT THE AUTHOR

Donald O. Dewey is Professor of History at California State College, Los Angeles. He has been an Associate Editor of *The Papers of James Madison* at the University of Chicago. Professor Dewey is the author of *Union and Liberty* (1969) and coeditor of *The Continuing Dialogue* (1965). He is a contributor to numerous professional journals.

A NOTE ON THE TYPE

This book was set on the Linotype in Baskerville. The punches for this face were cut under the supervision of George W. Jones, the eminent English printer and the designer of Granjon and Estienne. Linotype Baskerville is a facsimile cutting from type cast from the original matrices of a face designed by John Baskerville, a writing master of Birmingham, for his own private press. The original face was the forerunner of the "modern" group of type faces, known today as Scotch, Bodoni, etc. After his death in 1775, Baskerville's punches and matrices were sold in France and were used to produce the sumptuous Kehl edition of Voltaire's works.

This book was composed by Cherry Hill Composition; printed and bound by Halliday Lithograph Corp., West Hanover, Mass.

Series Design by J. M. Wall